Collins

Maths Now

2

Author
Prabha Sethy

Student + Teacher		Teacher-only
a animations	**ia** activities	**lp** lesson plans
ilt instructor-led tutorials	**w** worksheets	**w** worksheets
g games	**v** videos	**tn** teacher's notes
		ak answer keys

Preface

Maths Now is a series of eight books for classes 1 to 8 based on the NCERT syllabus. The series follows an activity-oriented approach to make mathematics engaging for students through emphasizing connections between mathematics and day-to-day experiences. This series also features the balanced use of manipulatives, virtual manipulatives, abstract ideas and other interesting features to improve inherent mathematical skills of students by creating foundational interest in the subject.

This series has been created with a view to enhance the students' understanding of the key concepts of mathematical problem-solving and to increase practical learning by bringing in contexts from outside the classroom. The main aim of the series is to eradicate maths phobia among students, make mathematical concepts crystal clear so that students appreciate the beauty of the subject and the role it plays in one's life.

Key Features

Let's Get Started Chapter starter in the form of a picture-based exercise

Mental Maths Objective-type questions to develop quick-thinking skills

Go Easy! Additional tips helping students to calculate quickly

Do You Know? Nuggets of information to add real-world context to abstract mathematical concepts

Common Errors Pointers highlighting common mistakes and misconceptions

Solved Examples Exercises with step-by-step solutions

Word Problems Textual questions based on real-life situations

Exercises In-text objective-type questions for quick review

Crossword and Puzzles Mathematical problems to stimulate the students' engagement

Maths Lab Activity Hands-on activity to connect concepts with their practical uses in real-life situations

Concept Map Graphic organizer to logically represent relationships between concepts under one topic

Key Concepts List to concisely give an overview of concepts in each topic

Chapter Revision Exercises at the end of each chapter for a comprehensive review

Skill Up!

- **Project** Practical activities to enhance real-world application of concepts
- **Life Skills** Questions to inculcate positive behaviour and add a layer of ethical thinking while solving practical mathematical questions
- **Mind Buzzer** Questions to provide challenging questions relating to real-life examples

Teacher's Notes Important tips related to concepts for the teacher

Worksheets Exercises that covers financial literacy, inferential and experiential learning

Reasoning Worksheet Questions to stimulate rational thinking using mathematical skills

Eminent Mathematicians Brief write-up on eminent mathematicians and their contributions

Poster Important points and formulae in the form of a pull-out page

Review Corner Variety of questions at the end of the book for additional practice

We would like to take this opportunity to thank all the teachers who reviewed the books and provided their feedback, which helped in improving the quality of the content.

Feedback, invaluable comments and suggestions from users are welcome.

Authors

Key Features

Different features interspersed within the book aim to provide active learning tools and techniques. These tools and techniques have been designed keeping in mind the 5E principle based on the constructivist approach to learning. These features can be used as learning strategies to enhance the understanding of key concepts of mathematics and increase practical learning and problem-solving by bringing in real-life contexts from outside the classroom.

Engage: To capture the attention of students, become mentally engaged and make connections between past and present knowledge

- Let's Get Started
- Common Errors
- Go Easy!
- Vedic Maths (classes 6 to 8)
- Eminent Mathematicians
- Poster

Explore: To enable the students to explore the concepts through hands-on activities, investigations, etc.

- Maths Lab Activity
- Crosswords
- Puzzles
- Mental Maths

Explain: To enable the students to understand the main ideas of the topics

- Learning Objectives
- Note
- Solved Examples
- Concept Map
- Key Concepts

Extend: To enable the students to stimulate thinking and apply prior and current knowledge to real-life situations

- Do You Know?
- Word Problems
- Skill Up!
  - Project
  - Life Skills
  - Mind Buzzer

Evaluate: To review, assess and evaluate what students have learnt

- Exercises
- Chapter Revision
- Reasoning Worksheet
- Worksheet
- Review Corner

Balanced use of Manipulatives, Virtual Manipulatives and Abstract Ideas!

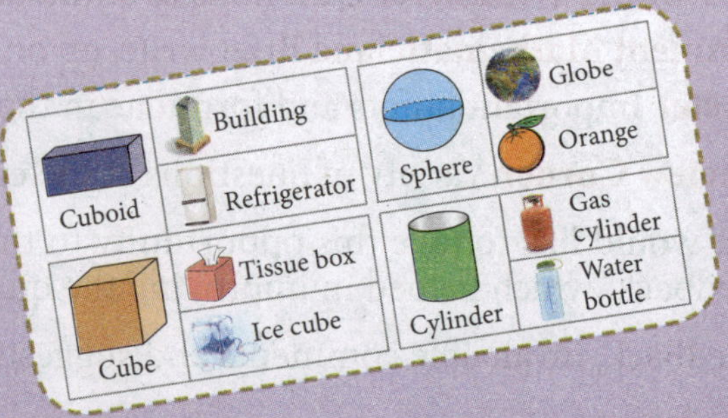

About the Features

Engage

Let's Get Started
Picture-based chapter-opening exercise

Common Errors
Pointers highlighting common mistakes and misconceptions

Eminent Mathematicians
Brief write-up on eminent mathematicians and their contributions

Go Easy!
Shortcuts for easy and fast calculations

VEDIC MATHS
Shortcut techniques to solve mathematical calculations

Poster
Important points and formulae in the form of a pull-out page

Explore

Maths Lab Activity
Hands-on activity to help in improving investigation, reinforcement and extension of concepts just learnt

Mental Maths
Objective-type questions to develop quick-thinking skills

PUZZLE!
Questions in the form of a puzzle to stimulate engagement with the concepts

CROSSWORD
Questions in the form of a crossword to stimulate engagement with the concepts

Explain

Note
Pointers for better understanding of concepts

SOLVED EXAMPLES
Example exercises with step-by-step solutions

Concept Map
Logical representation of relationships between concepts in a chapter

Key Concepts
- Definition of important terms and formulae given as bulleted list

Extend

Do you know?
Nuggets of information to add real-world context to abstract mathematical concepts

WORD PROBLEMS
Textual questions based on real-life situations

SKILL UP!

Project
Practical activities to enhance real-world application of concepts

Life Skills
Thought-provoking questions to help develop sensible life skills such as better awareness, empathy and attitude towards self and others

Mind Buzzer
Questions to arouse intellectual curiosity and encourage the students to think beyond the classroom

Evaluate

EXERCISE
In-text objective-type questions for quick review, assessment and evaluation

Chapter Revision
Chapter-end questions with varieties of objective and subjective-type questions

REASONING WORKSHEET
Questions to stimulate rational thinking using mathematical skills

WORKSHEET
Picture-based, fun problem-solving questions to reinforce concepts

REVIEW CORNER
Variety of questions at the end of the book for additional practice

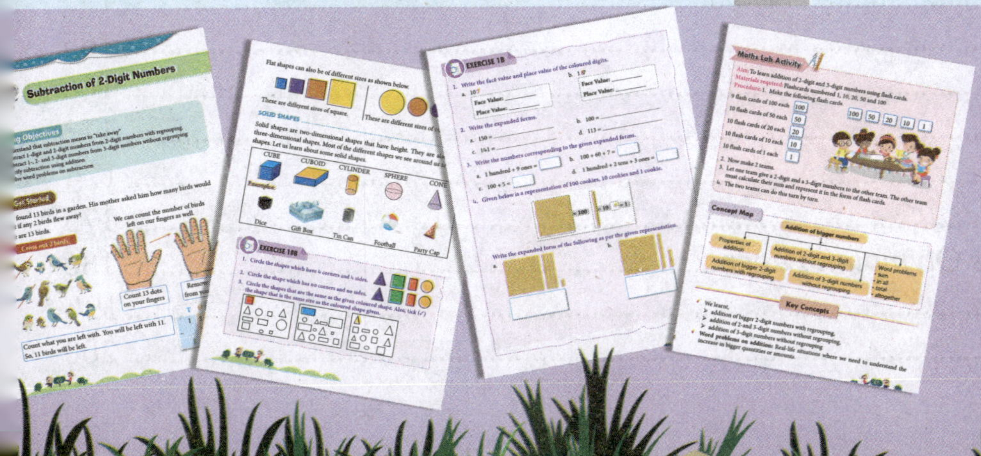

Maths Around Us
A two-page feature providing a variety of interesting information and activities that connect maths and Indian history, art, culture, real-life situations and financial literacy

Contents

Maths Around Us

COLOURS, SHAPES AND PATTERNS OF LEAVES

Do you know that by looking at the colour of some leaves, we can identify the season?

Here are some leaves that change colour across different seasons in a year. Maple and birch are examples of such trees whose leaves change colour from one season to another.

Maple trees look the most beautiful in autumn. In spring, the leaves are reddish in colour. In summer, the leaves are usually green. In autumn, the colour of the leaves changes to many shades of orange, yellow and brown.

Do you know which country's flag has maple leaf as a symbol?

You can also observe different patterns in leaves.

Look around your neighbourhood or locality. Are there any trees whose leaves change colour according to different seasons? Collect such leaves and paste in the space provided below. Write a few lines about the colour and the pattern of the leaves.

Paste the leaves here.

1 Numbers up to 200

Learning Objectives

- To read, write and compare numbers up to 200 and write their number names
- To understand the face value, place value and expanded form
- To learn the order of numbers, ascending/descending and even/odd numbers
- To learn ordinal numbers

Let's Get Started

1. Write the numbers given below in descending order inside the balloons. (left to right) 98, 45, 23, 67, 12
2. Write the numbers and the number names corresponding to the numbers in pink, purple, blue and green balloons.

   a. ______ = ____________________ b. ______ = ____________________

   c. ______ = ____________________ d. ______ = ____________________
3. The balloon with the smallest number is ________ in colour.
4. The balloon with the greatest number is ________ in colour.
5. The blue balloon is placed just after the ________ balloon.
6. The orange balloon is placed just before the ________ balloon.
7. Compare the numbers in green and pink balloons using > or <.

   ________ ☐ ________
8. Blue balloon is in between ________ and ________ balloons.

INTRODUCTION TO NUMBERS UP TO 200

We have learnt the numbers from 1 to 99 in previous class.

When 1 is added to 99, we get a 3-digit number, that is, 100.

99 + 1 = **100**

The two zeros are written under Ones and Tens and 1 is written under Hundreds.

We can write it as:

Hundreds	Tens	Ones
H	T	O
1	0	0

Note
100 is the smallest 3-digit number.

Numbers from 101 to 200

Let us have a look at the 3-digit numbers from 101 to 200.

101	102	103	104	105	106	107	108	109	110
111	112	113	114	115	116	117	118	119	120
121	122	123	124	125	126	127	128	129	130
131	132	133	134	135	136	137	138	139	140
141	142	143	144	145	146	147	148	149	150
151	152	153	154	155	156	157	158	159	160
161	162	163	164	165	166	167	168	169	170
171	172	173	174	175	176	177	178	179	180
181	182	183	184	185	186	187	188	189	190
191	192	193	194	195	196	197	198	199	200

Go Easy!
Word form of a number is same as its number name. Short form of a word form is the numeral itself.

Note
Each number given inside this grid is 1 more than the previous number.

Nick loves to eat cookies. He buys at least 2 to 3 packs of 10 cookies each time he visits the market. Let us see how many cookies he bought.

1 packet = 10 cookies. How many cookies will there be in 10 packets?

Using repeated addition, we must add 10, ten times.

10 + 10 + 10 + 10 + 10 + 10 + 10 + 10 + 10 + 10 = **100 cookies**

100 cookies can be shown as,

The two zeros are written under Ones and Tens and 1 is written under Hundreds.

He also bought 1 loose cookie, so now we add 100 and 1, we get,

	H	T	O
	1	0	0
+			1
	1	0	1

cookies

So, Nick purchased **101** cookies. It is read as '**one hundred one**'. This can be shown using cookies as given below.

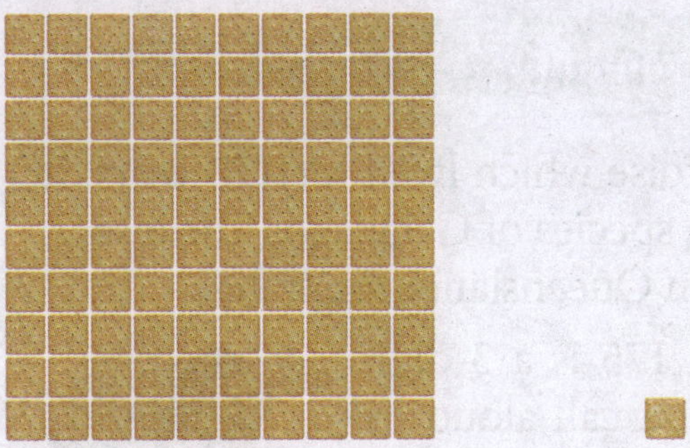

= 101

1 hundred One

Number name of 101 = One hundred one

Let us learn more about 3-digit numbers.

While reading a 3-digit number, the number at the tens and the ones place is read and spoken together. So, 156 is read as One hundred **fifty-six**.

Now, consider the following set of cookies.

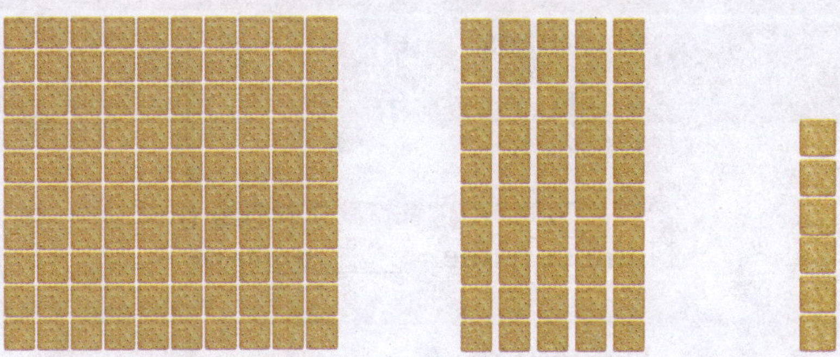

1 hundred 5 tens 6 ones

=

H	T	O
1	5	6

Number name of 156
= One hundred fifty-six

Let us understand the number 200 by considering the following sets of cookies.

The number 200 comes just after 199. It will have 2 sets of hundred cookies.

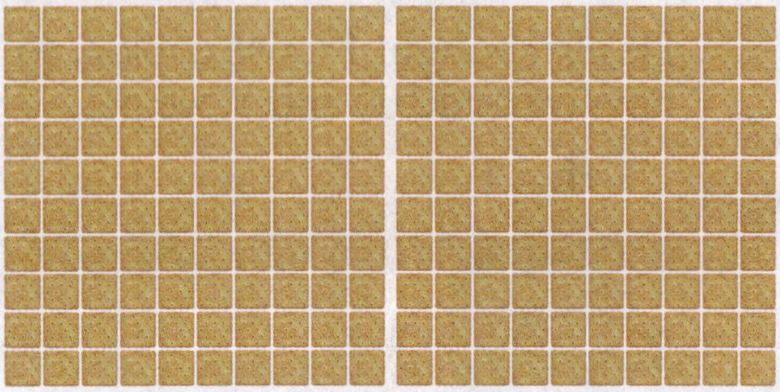

2 hundreds

=

H	T	O
2	0	0

Number name of 200
= Two hundred

Similarly, we can also read and write other 3-digit numbers like 102, 103, 104, 111, 112, 132, 144, 147, 161, 179, and so on.

Note

Predecessor: is the number just before a given number.

Example: 123 is predecessor of 124.

Successor: is the number just after a given number.

Example: 192 is successor of 191.

Do you know?

Harriet is a tortoise which lived for 175 years. It belonged to the species of Galapagos Tortoise. It was last found in Queensland, Australia.

As we observe, 175 is a 3-digit number. Can you call aloud its number name?

EXERCISE 1A

1. Fill in the blanks.

a.

Hundreds Ones

Hundreds H	Tens T	Ones O

Number name = ____________

b.

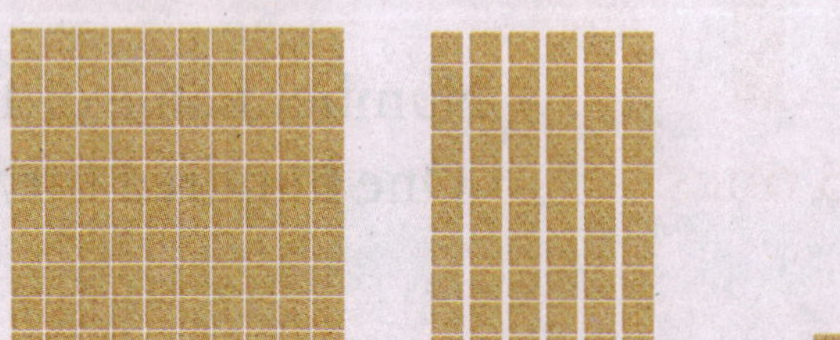

Hundreds Tens Ones

Hundreds H	Tens T	Ones O

Number name = ____________

2. **Write the numerals of the following.**

a. One hundred seventy [ ] b. One hundred eighty-seven [ ]

3. **Write the number names of the following.**

a. 143 = ____________________

b. 155 = ____________________

4. **Match the following.**

Column A

H	T	O
1	3	5
1	0	3
1	0	0
1	4	8
1	7	6

Column B

Number Names

One hundred

One hundred three

One hundred forty-eight

One hundred seventy-six

One hundred thirty-five

5. **Complete the grid from 151 to 200. Call aloud the number names.**

151									
	162							169	
				175	176				
181									190
			194			197			200

6. **Write the numbers just after:**

a. 161 [ ] b. 196 [ ]

7. **Write the numbers just before:**

a. [ ] 200 b. [ ] 127

8. **Complete the pattern.** 191, 190, [ ], [ ], [ ], [ ]

9. **What is the predecessor of 167?** [ ]

10. **What is the successor of 110?** [ ]

FACE VALUE AND PLACE VALUE

Each digit in a number contains a face value and a place value.

Face Value of a digit is the digit itself.

Place value of a digit is the face value of the digit multiplied by its place.
This shows the relationship between face value and place value.

> **Note**
> **Face value** of a digit cannot be changed.
> **Place value** of a digit can be changed depending upon the place of the digit in the number.
> **Example:** Consider the numbers, 135 and 153.
> - Face value of 3 in both 135 and 153 is 3.
> - Place value of 3 in 135 is 30 and place value of 3 in 153 is 3.

A 1-digit number has one digit placed at the ones place.
Example 1: Consider the number 5. Face value of 5 is 5. Place value of 5 is 5.
A 2-digit number has two digits, placed at the tens and ones places respectively.

Example 2: The number 25.

Tens	Ones
2	5

Digits in the number 25	Face Value	Place Value
2	2	20
5	5	5

A 3-digit number has three digits, each placed at hundreds, tens and ones place respectively.

Example 3: The number 152.

Hundreds	Tens	Ones
1	5	2

Digits in the number 152	Face Value	Place Value
1	1	100
5	5	50
2	2	2

EXPANDED FORM

The expanded form of a number is written as an addition statement of the place values of all the digits. Consider the place value of the digits of the number 148 in the given table.

<table>
<tr><th>Digits in the number 148</th><th>Place Value</th><th>Expanded form</th></tr>
<tr><td>1</td><td>100</td><td rowspan="3">100 + 40 + 8 or 1 hundred + 4 tens + 8 ones</td></tr>
<tr><td>4</td><td>40</td></tr>
<tr><td>8</td><td>8</td></tr>
</table>

EXERCISE 1B

1. **Write the face value and place value of the coloured digits.**

   a. 107

   Face Value: __________

   Place Value: __________

   b. 187

   Face Value: __________

   Place Value: __________

2. **Write the expanded forms.**

   a. 150 = ____________________

   b. 100 = ____________________

   c. 141 = ____________________

   d. 113 = ____________________

3. **Write the numbers corresponding to the given expanded forms.**

   a. 1 hundred + 9 ones = [ ]

   b. 100 + 60 + 7 = [ ]

   c. 100 + 5 = [ ]

   d. 1 hundred + 2 tens + 3 ones = [ ]

4. **Given below is a representation of 100 cookies, 10 cookies and 1 cookie.**

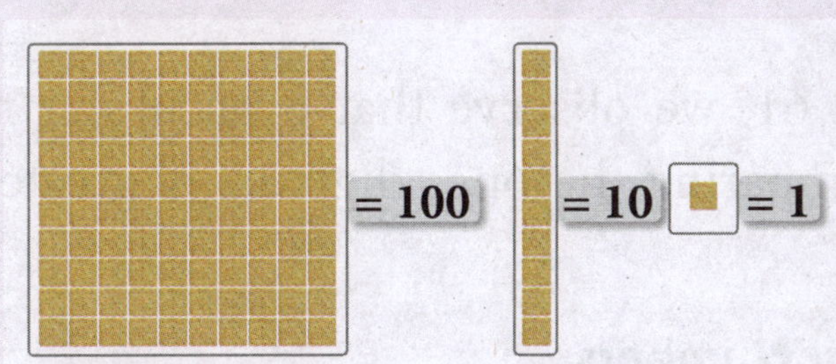

Write the expanded form of the following as per the given representation.

a.

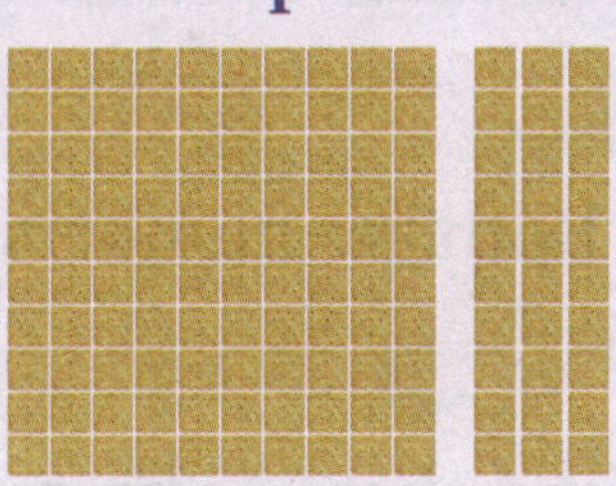

[ ]

b.

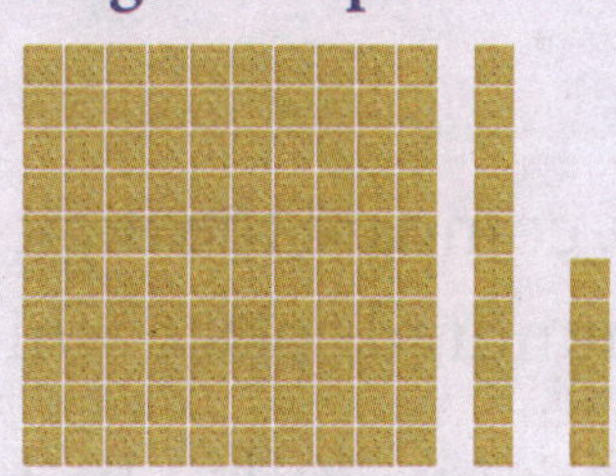

[ ]

NUMBER COMPARISON

We have learnt about less than, greater than and equal to symbols in class 1.

Symbol for Less than is **<** | Symbol for Greater than is **>**

Symbol for Equal to is **=**

When we compare numbers, we find out whether a number is greater than or less than or equal to another number.

Comparing a 3-Digit Number and a 2-Digit Number

Compare 193 and 99.

The number with lesser number of digits is smaller.

So, 99 < 193 or 193 > 99

Comparing Two 2-Digit Numbers

Compare 57 and 75.

Compare the digits in the tens place. 5 is less than 7.

So, 57 < 75 or 75 > 57

If the Digits at the Tens Place are Same, then Compare the Digits at the Ones Place.

If we compare 68 and 61, we observe that 6 occurs at the tens place in both the numbers. Then comparing the ones digits, 8 is greater than 1. Hence, 68 is greater than 61.

Comparing Two 3-Digit Numbers

Compare 153 and 127.

Steps:

1. First, compare the digits in the hundreds place. Both the numbers have 1 in the hundreds place which is the same.
2. Now compare the digits in the tens place. We find that 5 is greater than 2. So, 153 > 127.

- If the digits at both the hundreds and tens place are equal, then compare the digits at the ones place. For example, compare 139 and 134. Here, 1 and 3 occur at the hundreds and tens place respectively, in both the numbers. Comparing the digits at the ones place, we find that 9 is greater than 4. So, 139 > 134.

Mental Maths

1. Write the short form of one hundred eleven. ____________
2. Write the number name of 184. ____________________________________
3. Write the face value and the place value of 9 in 149. ____________, ____________
4. Write the number that comes just before 149. ____________
5. Write the expanded form of 116. ________________

EXERCISE 1C

1. Tick (✔) the greater number.

a. 135 ☐ 133 ☐ b. 200 ☐ 172 ☐

c. 111 ☐ 100 ☐ d. 165 ☐ 156 ☐

2. Circle the smallest number.

a. 133, 122, 111 b. 111, 109, 191

c. 122, 169, 154 d. 151, 180, 116

3. Compare the digits using >, < or =.

a. 175 ☐ 185 b. 146 ☐ 144 c. 198 ☐ 200 d. 153 ☐ 153

4. Colour the greatest number.

a. 144 134 194 b. 107 108 105

c. 147 144 142 d. 161 188 195

ORDER OF NUMBERS

The teacher in a classroom placed five paper chits on her table. She wrote down 5 random numbers on these 5 chits. Then she asked 5 students to pick up the chits without looking at them.

Nick, Khilee, Kavya, Radhika and Sam picked up the chits and the numbers written on them are shown in the picture on the following page.

They are standing in order of the numbers from smallest to the greatest. This shows that they are standing in **increasing or ascending order** of the numbers picked by them. That is, 17, 95, 137, 160, 199

However, when they stand from right to left, that is Sam, Radhika, Kavya, Khilee and Nick, the order of numbers becomes greatest to smallest. This is known as the **decreasing or descending order**.

That is, 199, 160, 137, 95, 17

EXERCISE 1D

1. **Arrange the following in ascending order.**
   a. 130, 10, 155, 166, 110, 190 ____________
   b. 111, 151, 189, 107, 170, 45 ____________

2. **Arrange the following in descending order.**
   a. 199, 200, 191, 198, 192, 195 ____________
   b. 188, 108, 118, 181, 110, 106 ____________

ORDINAL NUMBERS

Ordinal numbers help us to refer to the positions of numbers. We use the following terms:

First for 1, Second for 2, Third for 3 and so on.

Ordinal numbers from 1 to 10 are given below.

Position:	1	2	3	4	5
Ordinal:	First	Second	Third	Fourth	Fifth
Written as:	1st	2nd	3rd	4th	5th

Position:	6	7	8	9	10
Ordinal:	Sixth	Seventh	Eighth	Ninth	Tenth
Written as:	6th	7th	8th	9th	10th

EXERCISE 1E

1. Before going for a birthday party, Sunny placed his outfit to wear on the bed in a sequence. The sequence is given below.

Answer the following.

a.  is the ____________ (first/third) item placed on the bed.

b. At what time, he wished to wear his  ? ____________ (first/third)

c. It was winter season. So, Sunny picked up the ____________ (second/fifth) item to wear.

d. Which item did he wear around his neck? It is the ____________ (third/fourth) item in sequence.

e. He wishes to wear the trousers in the end. State true or false. ____________.

f. He has placed the trousers at the ____________ (first/second) position.

2. There are 26 letters in English alphabet. The first 10 letters are given below.

A B C D E F G H I J

a. Which is the second letter? ____________

b. G comes just after F. G is the ____________ letter. (sixth/seventh)

c. Write the tenth letter ____________. Which letter is just before the tenth letter? ____________

d. Name and write the colour of the fifth letter. ____________

e. C comes in between ____________ and ____________. The letter C is at the ____________ position. (third/fifth)

EVEN AND ODD NUMBERS

One Pair = 2 Objects

What are **pairs of objects?**

When two objects are placed together, they are considered as one pair.

Consider the following objects around you that occur in pairs.

a pair of shoes

a pair of socks

a pair of gloves

a pair of earrings

This shows that things that occur in **pairs** are basically **groups of two objects.**

We also have pairs of organs in human body like 2 eyes, 2 ears, 2 hands, 2 legs, 2 feet, 2 arms, 2 lungs, etc.

Consider a pair of earrings.

One pair has **2** earrings.

Now consider, two pairs of earrings.

Two pairs have **4** earrings.

Three pairs of earrings is shown below.

Three pairs have **6** earrings.

Four pairs of earrings is shown below.

Four pairs have **8** earrings.

Five pairs of earrings is shown below.

Five pairs have **10** earrings.

Numbers that can be divided into groups of two are **even numbers**. An **even number** is a number whose last digit is 0, 2, 4, 6 or 8.
Examples: 32, 54, 126, 178, 190

Numbers that cannot be divided into groups of two are **odd numbers**. An **odd number** is a number whose last digit is 1, 3, 5, 7 or 9.
Examples: 21, 63, 145, 187, 129

Common Errors

1. 012 ✗ 120 ✓
   A number cannot start with 0.
2. Ordinal numbers:
   4th = Forth ✗ Fourth ✓
   9th = Nineth ✗ Ninth ✓
3. Number names:
   40
   fourty ✗ forty ✓
   19
   Ninteen ✗ Nineteen ✓

EXERCISE 1F

1. **Out of the numbers given, write all the even numbers in House A and all the odd numbers in House B.**

   125 21 150 142 4 160 194 161

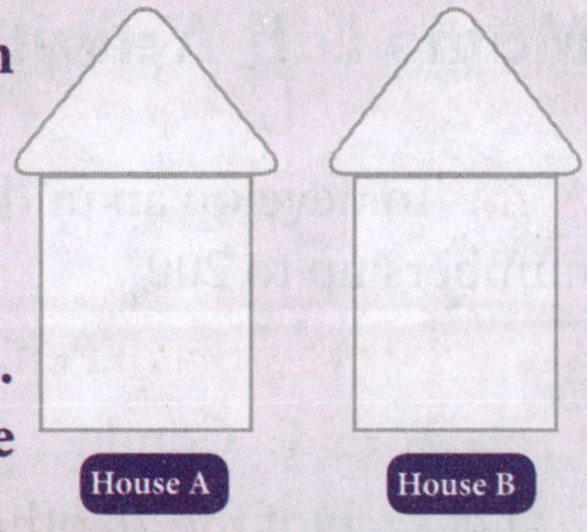

2. **Group the following shapes by circling them in pairs. Count the total and check whether it is even or odd. One has been done for you.**

a. 

b. 

c. 

d. 

e. 

f. 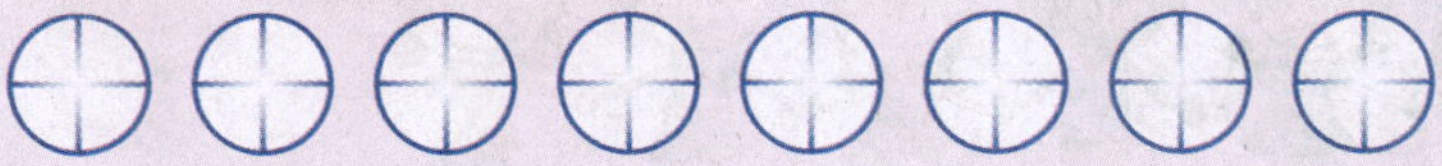

	Number	Even/Odd
a.	5	Odd
b.		
c.		
d.		
e.		
f.		

3. **Circle the objects that occur in pairs.**

Mental Maths

1. Both Kanu and Renu have 1 rupee coins. Kanu has 110 coins and Renu has 125 coins. Who has more money? __________
2. Fill in the blanks.
   a. 145 is ____________ than 140. b. 190 is ____________ 191.
3. Write T for true and F for false.
   a. 124 > 170 ____________
   b. One hundred eleven is word form of 101. ____________
   c. 199 is an even number.
   d. The place value of 1 in 132 is 10. ____________

Maths Lab Activity

Aim: To develop an understanding of numbers, number names and expanded forms of numbers up to 200

Materials required: Pen, notebook

Procedure: 1. Conduct an activity by assigning numbers from 1 to 9 each to nine students.

2. Let each of the 20 other students be assigned the number, 10.
3. The teacher calls out the number, 48. The students gather together as shown below.

4 students with the number 10 and 1 student with the number 8 gather together.

10 10 10 10 8 = 48

4. Similarly, try forming other numbers such as 125 as shown below.

10 10 10 10 10 10 10 10 10 10 = 100

10 10 = 20

5 = 5

Adding 100, 20 and 5, we get 125.

5. Now the teacher asks one student to give the number names and the expanded forms of the numbers just called out.

Conclusion: With the help of this activity, students can learn how to call aloud numbers up to 200.

Concept Map

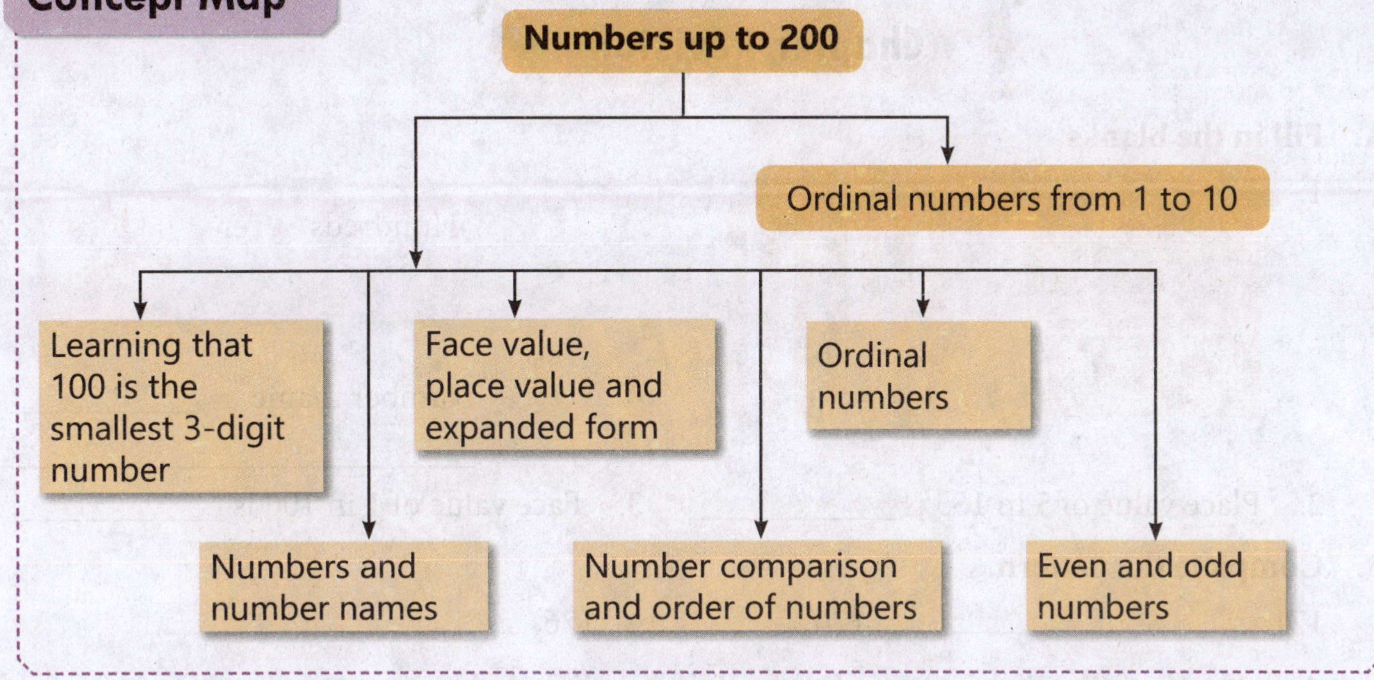

Key Concepts

- **One hundred:** The smallest 3-digit number, written as 100.
- **Number name:** The name of a number expressed in words.
- **Face value:** Face value of a digit is the digit itself.
- **Place value:** The value of each digit in a number.
- **Expanded form:** The expanded form of a number is written as an addition statement of the place values of all the digits.
- **Comparing number:** To find out whether a number is greater than or less than or equal to another number.
- **Ascending/Descending order:** Arranging numbers from smallest to greatest is ascending/increasing order and arranging numbers from greatest to smallest is descending/decreasing order.
- **Even and odd numbers:** Even numbers end with 2, 4, 6, 8 or 0 and odd numbers end with 1, 3, 5, 7 or 9.
- **Ordinal numbers:** refer to the positions of numbers like first, second, third and so on.

Chapter Revision

A. Fill in the blanks.

1.

Hundreds	Tens	Ones

Number name = ____________

____

2. Place value of 5 in 153 is __________. 3. Face value of 1 in 100 is __________.

B. Complete the pattern.

171, ________, ________, 174, ________, 176, ________, ________.

C. Arrange the following in ascending and descending order.

Numbers	Ascending Order	Descending Order
1. 181, 175, 166, 109, 190		
2. 111, 101, 110, 114, 117		

D. Sid placed all his birthday gifts in a row.

Fill in the blanks.

1. Sid's favourite gift is placed second in the row. What is his favourite gift? ________
2. His best friend gave him the third gift. What did his best friend give him? ________
3. Sid loved the colour of the t-shirt. It is placed at the ________ position in the row.
4. Sid felt excited to show his ________ gift, that is, his new school bag to his friends.
5. His mother gave him the bicycle. Sid placed it at the ________ position in the row.

E. Place the even numbers in Bag A and odd numbers in Bag B.

200 49 5 136 140 18 192 165 100 62 178

Bag A

Bag B

SKILL UP!

Project

1. Collect buttons in 7 different colours. 

   Specify the colours of these buttons along with the ordinals.

2. Find out the date of 150th birth anniversary of Mahatma Gandhi in the year 2019. 150 is a 3-digit number. Call aloud the number name and expanded form of 150.

Life Skills

Flat no. 3, 4th floor,
Tower 116, Tank Road

Sarika's home address is given alongside.

a. Which ordinal number is used in the address? __________
   Is it used for the flat number or the floor number? __________
b. The flat number is less than the floor number. True or False. __________.
c. Is the tower number an even number or an odd number? __________
d. How will you express the tower number in words? ____________________

Mind Buzzer

1. Consider the grid of numbers from 101 to 200 given on page 2. Write down the numerals and the number names of the numbers where
   a. the digits at the ones place is zero
   b. the digits at the tens place and ones place are same
2. Write all the possible 3-digit numbers from 100 to 200 using the digits 0, 4, 9 and 1 only once. Arrange them in descending order.

Teacher's Notes

- Collecting 200 beads or buttons or 200 one rupee coins will give them an idea about the quantity of numbers till 200.
- Practice exercises always help to understand the concepts like place value, face value, expanded form, etc.
- Children can make groups of odd and even numbers to understand the concept of even and odd or to know less than/greater than or ascending/descending arrangements.
- 10 children can stand in a line and the teacher can call out to the first, second or third child till the tenth child to practise ordinals.

WORKSHEET

1. Label the objects from first to tenth. One has been done for you. Draw lines from the objects to the boxes (A to E) that they belong to as per the instructions given.

1st				

Instructions

Draw lines as:

First and eighth item - Box A

Fifth and ninth item - Box B

Sixth and tenth item - Box C

Second and seventh item - Box D

Third and fourth item - Box E

A	B	C	D	E

2. Fill in the following crossword as per the instructions given.

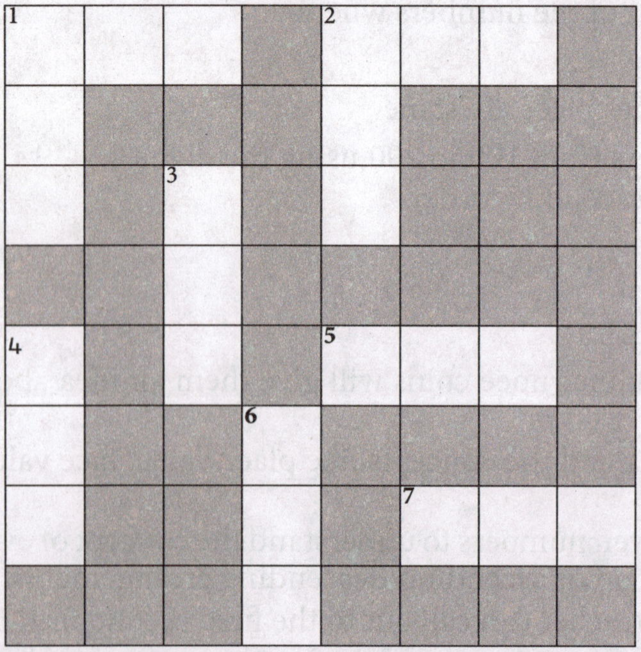

Across

1. One hundred three
2. One hundred twenty-four
5. One hundred sixty-nine
7. One hundred ninety-eight

Down

1. One hundred twelve
2. One hundred thirty-five
3. One hundred forty-six
4. One hundred fifty
6. One hundred seventy-two

2 Addition of 2-Digit Numbers

Learning Objectives

- To understand the addition of 1-digit and 2-digit numbers with 2-digit numbers (with and without regrouping)
- To understand the addition of three 2-digit numbers (with and without regrouping)
- To learn how to verify addition
- To learn the properties of addition and solving word problems

Let's Get Started

It is Annual Day in school. Let us see the participation of students of class 2 in a few activities listed below.

Activity	Number of children participated
Singing	6
Dancing	5
Drawing	5
Swimming	7

What was the total number of students who participated?

WHAT IS ADDITION?

We add when we have to find the sum.

When we add, the value of something is going to increase by the given amount.

The sign of addition is ✚, read as 'plus'.

> **Note**
> a. To add means to put things together.
> b. Addition is counting forward.

Addition Facts

1. When we add 1 to a number, we get the number just after it.

   5 + 1 = 6   73 + 1 = 74

2. When we add 0 to a number, the value of the number does not change.

   143 + 0 = 143   199 + 0 = 199

3. The result of the sum of two numbers is the same when the order of numbers is changed.

   2 + 3 = 5; 3 + 2 = 5

   5 + 4 = 9; 4 + 5 = 9

Mental Maths

1. 4 + 1 = ______
2. 93 + 0 = ______
3. 4 + 1 = 1 + ___ = ___

PUZZLE!

Match the space ships with their creatures.

EXERCISE 2A

1. Add the following.

a. 8 + 0 = ____   b. 54 + 1 = ____   c. 83 + 0 = ____   d. 136 + 1 = ____

2. Add the following.

a. 0 + 5 = ____   b. 3 + 7 = 7 + ____ = ____   c. 4 + 3 = 3 + ____ = ____

ADDITION OF 1-DIGIT AND 2-DIGIT NUMBERS

This includes:

- Addition of 1-digit numbers with 2-digit numbers (with regrouping)
- Addition of two 2-digit numbers (with regrouping)
- Addition of three 1-digit numbers
- Addition of three 2-digit numbers (with and without regrouping)

Addition of 1-Digit Numbers with 2-Digit Numbers with regrouping

We learnt about adding two 1-digit numbers and 1-digit with 2-digit numbers without carrying forward in class 1.

Let us see how we can add a 1-digit number with a 2-digit number with regrouping.

Example: Kanu bought 15 doughnuts. Meenu bought 8 doughnuts. Find the total number of doughnuts.

Solution: 15 is a 2-digit number and 8 is a 1-digit number. We must add 15 and 8 to find the total number of doughnuts.

Step 1: Add the digits in the ones place.

	T	O
	1	
	1	5
+		8
		3

15 has 1 ten and 5 ones.
8 has 8 ones.
Step 1: Add the ones
So, 5 ones + 8 ones = 13 ones.
Write 3 of 13 in the ones place and carry over 1 of 13 to the tens place as shown.

Step 2: Add the digits in tens place.

	T	O
	1	
	1	5
+		8
	2	3

Step 2: Add the tens
The carried over 1 is added to the 1 of 15 to give 2 in the tens place.

The total number of doughnuts are **23**.

Common Errors

Place the one-digit number under the ones column always.

	T	O
	3	5
+	3	

✗

	T	O
	3	5
+		3

✓

	T	O
	1	
	4	6
+	2	4
	6	0

✗

	T	O
	1	
	4	6
+	2	4
	7	0

✓

	T	O
	3	5
+	1	5
	4 1	0

✗

	T	O
	1	
	3	5
+	1	5
	5	0

✓

Addition of Two 2-Digit Numbers with Regrouping

Radhika had two necklaces. The red necklace had 39 beads and the blue necklace had 15 beads. How many beads are there in all?

Since we have to find the number of beads in all, so we must add.

Step 1:

	T	O
	1	
	3	9
+	1	5
		4

In the ones column, 9 + 5 = 14. Now 14 is a 2-digit number, so we write '4' of 14 in the ones column and carry forward '1' of 14 and place it on top of 3 in the tens column.

Step 1:

	T	O
	1	
	3	9
+	1	5
	5	4

Now add all the tens digits in the tens column, 1 + 3 + 1 = 5.

Write 5 in the tens column.

There are 54 beads in all.

EXERCISE 2B

1. Regroup and add the following.

a.

	T	O
		6
+		5

b.

	T	O
	3	8
+	5	6

c.

	T	O
		7
+		4

d.

	T	O
	4	6
+	3	6

2. Find the sum.

a. 5 tens + 2 tens + 3 ones ______

b. 1 tens + 8 tens ______

c. 4 tens + 5 ones ______

d. 2 tens + 6 tens + 4 ones ______

ADDITION OF THREE 1-DIGIT NUMBERS

1. When we add three 1-digit numbers, we first add two digits and then add the third digit to the sum of first two digits.

Example 1: Solve 2 + 3 + 4.

1. 2 + 3 + 4

Solution: 2 + 3 + 4.

First solve 2 + 3.

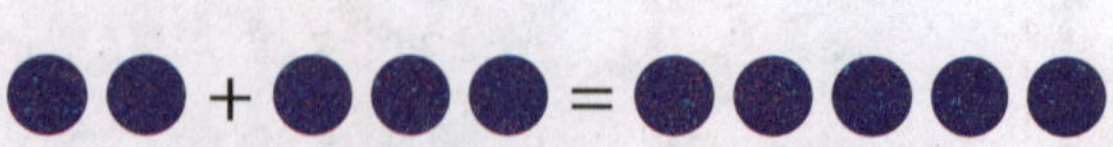

We get 5. Now solve 5 + 4.

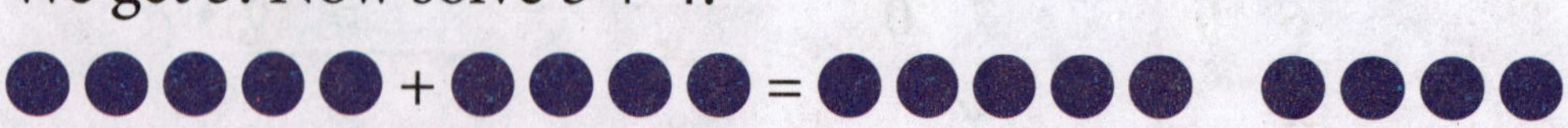

Thus, 5 + 4 = 9. So, 2 + 3 + 4 = 9

2. While adding three numbers, we should check if the sum of any two numbers is 10. If it is, then it becomes easier if we add the third number to 10 to get the answer.

Example 2: Solve 6 + 4 + 3.

6 + 4 + 3 (6 + 4 bracketed)

10 + 3

6 + 4 + 3 = **13**

6 + 4 = **10**

10 + 3 = **13**

We can do this vertically too.

$$\begin{array}{r} 6 \\ 4 \\ +\ 3 \\ \hline \end{array} \quad (6 + 4 = 10) \qquad \begin{array}{r} 10 \\ +\ 3 \\ \hline \mathbf{13} \\ \hline \end{array}$$

ADDITION OF THREE 2-DIGIT NUMBERS WITHOUT REGROUPING

Rita bought 15 balloons, 23 party hats and 11 ice cream cones. How many items did she buy in all?

Number of balloons =

Number of party hats =

Number of ice cream cones =

In the ones column, 5 + 3 + 1 = **9**

Write 9 in the ones column.

	T	O
	1	5
	2	3
+	1	1
		9

	T	O
	1	5
	2	3
+	1	1
	4	9

In the tens column, 1 + 2 + 1 = 4

Write 4 in the tens column.

Thus, Rita bought 49 items in all.

Note

We know that,

30 = 3 tens, 40 = 4 tens

So, we have,

30 + 40 = 3 tens + 4 tens

	T	O
	3	0
+	4	0
	7	0

= 7 tens

More Examples:

1.

	T	O
	3	2
	1	4
+	2	3
	6	9

2.

	T	O
	1	0
	2	5
+	4	3
	7	8

This is the case of addition of three 2-digit numbers without carrying forward or without regrouping. Now, we will learn addition of three 2-digit numbers with regrouping.

ADDITION OF THREE 2-DIGIT NUMBERS WITH REGROUPING

In a parking area, there were 26 cars, 49 scooters and 58 motorcycles. How many vehicles were there in all?

	T	O
Cars	2	6
Scooters	4	9
Motorcycles	+ 5	8
		3

In the ones column, 6 + 9 + 8 = **23**.

Write '3' of 23 in the ones column and carry forward '2' of 23 to the tens column.

Do you know?

Plus is a Latin word which means 'more'. Latin is a language used in Italy. Robert Recorde, who designed the equals sign, introduced the plus sign to Britain in the year 1557.

H	T	O
1	2	
	2	6
	4	9
+	5	8
1	3	3

Write '2' on the top of 1 in the tens column.

In the tens column,
2 + 2 + 4 + 5 = **13**. Write down 3 in the tens column and place 1 in the hundreds column.

Thus, there were 133 vehicles.

EXERCISE 2C

1. Add the following.

a.

O
4
1
+ 3

b.

O
3
2
+ 4

c.

T	O
	5
	5
+	7

d.

T	O
	7
	3
+	6

2. Regroup and add the following.

a.

T	O
1	2
3	4
+ 2	3

b.

T	O
2	5
3	0
+ 4	2

c.

T	O
3	1
2	4
+ 1	3

d.

T	O	
1	7	10
4	3	
+ 3	6	

VERIFYING ADDITION

We can check or verify addition by adding the numbers in the reverse order.

Examples:

1. Adding 39 and 22 will give the same result as adding 22 and 39.

	T	O
	1	
	3	9
+	2	2
	6	1

	T	O
	1	
	2	2
+	3	9
	6	1

2. Adding 12, 18 and 35 will give the same result as adding 35, 18 and 12.

	T	O
	1	
	1	2
	1	8
+	3	5
	6	5

	T	O
	1	
	3	5
	1	8
+	1	2
	6	5

EXERCISE 2D

Add and verify the solutions.

a.

	T	O
	3	4
+	4	8

Verify

T	O

b.

	T	O
	1	4
+	2	6

Verify

T	O

c.

	T	O
	8	4
+	1	9

Verify

T	O

d.

	T	O
	3	5
	4	5
+	1	5

Verify

T	O

Go Easy!

1. When we add the digits in the tens column (in case of carry forward to ten), the carried forward number must also be added with the tens digits.
2. Always start adding from the ones column.

WORD PROBLEMS

We add when we need to find the sum or total.

> **Note**
> Look out for addition words in a problem.
> **Addition Words:**
> Add, total, sum, plus, in all, altogether, more, increase, etc.

Example 1: 25 boys and 36 girls went to the park to play. How many children were there in all?

Solution:

		T	O
		1	
Boys		2	5
Girls	+	3	6
		6	1

Altogether, there were 61 children in the park.

Example 2: Radhika bought 66 sweets, 15 chocolates and 18 ice creams for her party. How many items did she buy at all?

	T	O
	1	
	6	6
	1	5
+	1	8
	9	9

Radhika bought 99 items in all.

EXERCISE 2E

1. The teacher distributed 25 English books and 41 Maths books to the children in the class. How many books did she distribute in all?

2. For Rajan's birthday party, his mother bought 58 samosas and 35 pizzas. What is the total number of samosas and pizzas that she bought?
3. Ritika read 46 pages of her book on Saturday and 38 pages of her book on Sunday. How many pages did she read on both these days?
4. A shopkeeper sold 48 blue pens, 10 black pens and 27 red pens in one day. What is the total number of pens he sold that day?

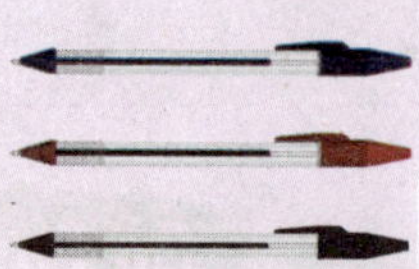

5. For the class picnic, the teacher bought 13 bottles of cola, 24 bottles of orange juice and 31 bottles of lemon juice. What was the total number of bottles that the teacher bought?

Mental Maths

1. 69 + ☐ = 70
2. 72 + 8 = ☐
3. 10 + 20 + 30 = ☐
4. 23 + 13 = 13 + ☐
5. The ones digit in the sum of 33 and 61 is ☐
6. 43 increased by 5 gives ☐
7. The next term in the series 11, 22, 33, 44, ☐, ☐.
8. 9 tens + 5 tens + 3 ones = ☐

PUZZLE!

Guess the number of children!

1. At 8 o'clock in the morning, 200 children of class 2 came to school.
2. At 9 o'clock, 32 more children of Class 2 entered the school.
3. By 10 o'clock, 121 more children entered the school premises, out of which 50 students belonged to class 2.

What is the total number of students in class 2? __________.

CROSSWORD

Study the clues given and fill in the crossword.

Across	Down
1. 62 + 43	1. 100 + 57
3. 69 + 5	2. 23 + 34
4. 125 + 63	5. 56 + 31
5. 25 + 63	6. 39 + 6
7. 38 + 15	8. 162 + 23
10. 45 + 54	9. 125 + 71
11. 70 + 10	11. 56 + 24

Maths Lab Activity

Aim: To reinforce the addition of 1-digit and 2-digit numbers with the help of currency notes

Materials required: Currency notes of 10, 20 and 50 and some coins of 1 rupee, 2 rupees and 5 rupees

Procedure: 1. Collect the following currency notes.

4 fifty-rupee notes 

10 twenty-rupee notes 

20 ten-rupees notes 

2. In how many ways can you make ₹50? One way is shown below. Think of two more ways for getting the sum as 50 using notes and coins of different denominations.

 +  +  = ₹50

How will you make ₹95 with the help of 10-rupee notes and one-rupee coins?

Concept Map

Addition of numbers upto 200

- Addition facts
- Addition of 1-digit and 2-digit numbers with regrouping
- Addition of 2-digit numbers with and without regrouping
- Addition of three 1-digit numbers
- Addition of three 2-digit numbers with and without regrouping
- Verifying addition
- Word problems
  - sum
  - in all
  - total
  - altogether

Key Concepts

- **Addition**: The process of adding numbers or finding the sum of numbers. Sum is another word used for addition, which means the result obtained after adding two numbers.
- **Carrying forward:** While carrying forward, we keep one part of the sum in the ones column and carry the other part to the tens column, to add it with numbers in the tens column. The concept is known as **regrouping**.
- **Addition facts:** Rules of addition. They are:
  - When we add 0 to a number, the value of the number does not change.
  - When we add 1 to a number, we get the number just after it.
  - We learnt addition of 1- and 2-digit numbers with 2-digit numbers with regrouping, addition of three 1-digit and three 2-digit numbers with regrouping.
- While verifying an addition problem, the numbers must be added in the reverse order again.
- **Word problems on addition:** Questions on application of addition based on our daily lives

Chapter Revision

A. Choose the correct option.

1. 18 + 22 is same as
   a. Forty-one b. Forty c. Forty-two d. Forty-three
2. Which two digits can be combined for easier addition in 4 + 2 + 6?
   a. 4 and 2 b. 4 and 6 c. 2 and 6
3. 22 + 33 + 27 gives the digit ___________ in the tens place.
   a. 9 b. 7 c. 8 d. 6

B. Match the following.

	Column A	Column B
1.	50 + 30	48 + 10 + 37
2.	20 + 21 + 35	17
3.	7 + 8 + 2	Thirty
4.	Ninety-five	35 + 21 + 20
5.	1 + 29	8 tens

C. Regroup and add.

1.

	T	O
	5	9
+		5

2.

	T	O
		6
		6
+		6

3.

	T	O
	3	7
	3	7
+	1	0

4.

	T	O
	4	9
+	1	7

D. Fill in the blanks:

1. 33 + 37 = ________
2. 4 tens + 7 tens = ________
3. The sum of 23 and 37 is ________
4. ________ is added to a number to get the next number.

E. Write T for true and F for false.

1. The number name for the sum of 20 and 36 is fifty-six. ☐
2. 15 + 0 + 1 = 15 ☐
3. When zero is added to a number, the answer is one more than the given number. ☐

F. Answer the following.

1. What is the sum of the smallest 2-digit number and greatest 2-digit number?
2. Karuna scored 30 marks, Sheena scored 35 marks and Tina scored 29 marks in a Mathematics test. What is the total marks scored by all of them?

SKILL UP!

Project

1. Find out the total number of students in two sections of class 2. Add the counts and find the total number of students.
2. Look at the sentence given below.

   'I love my Mathematics book very much'

   Write the number of vowels = ______

   Write the number of consonants = ______

   Add the vowels and the consonants.

	T	O
+		

Life Skills

Sumit, Nungsang and Raheem went to the park in the evening. Sumit ran 24 rounds of the park, Nungsang ran 20 rounds and Raheem ran 32 rounds. The children felt very good after the exercise and decided to do it every day.

What was the total number of rounds that all the three children took? Is it good to exercise everyday?

Mind Buzzer

1. If Samira had ₹125 and her mother gave her ₹38 more. How much money did Samira collect?
2. The ones digit and tens digit in the sum of two numbers are same. If one number is 24, what must be the other number to make the sum 66?

Teacher's Notes

- The children must know all the numbers from 1 to 200. Reading them aloud helps them to learn them.
- They must try addition using blocks, buttons or coins. It gives them clarity about the quantities till 200.
- Before solving addition problems, it is very important for the child to understand the problem and the operation used in it.
- The answer to every problem must be written in a sentence form.

WORKSHEET

Anu and Hazel went to a balloon seller. The balloon seller had numbered his balloons from 1 to 30. Each kid selected two sets of three balloons using the conditions given below.

a. Number on one balloon is the sum of the other two.

b. The sum is in between 20 and 30

c. The sum can be equal to 20 or 30.

Fill the blanks spaces inside the balloons with numbers selected by Anu and Hazel based on the conditions given.

Hint: **Observe the colour of the blank balloons. Identify the numbers corresponding to the colours from the list of balloons with numbers.**

Anu

Hazel

3 Subtraction of 2-Digit Numbers

Learning Objectives

- To understand that subtraction means to "take away"
- To subtract 1-digit and 2-digit numbers from 2-digit numbers with regrouping.
- To subtract 1-, 2- and 3-digit numbers from 3-digit numbers without regrouping
- To verify subtraction using addition
- To solve word problems on subtraction

Let's Get Started

A boy found 13 birds in a garden. His mother asked him how many birds would be left if any 2 birds flew away?

There are 13 birds.

Cross out 2 birds.

We can count the number of birds left on our fingers as well.

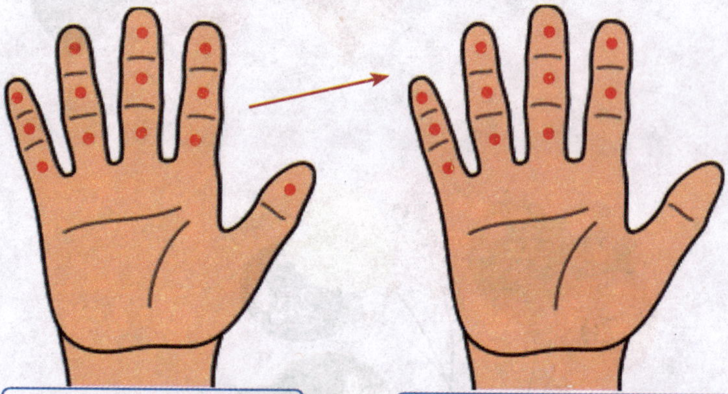

Count 13 dots on your fingers

Remove 2 dots from your fingers

Count what you are left with. You will be left with 11. So, 11 birds will be left.

	T	O
	1	3
–		2
	1	1

WHAT IS SUBTRACTION?

We subtract when,

- we have to take away some quantity from another quantity or
- the value of something is going to reduce by a given amount

The sign of subtraction is **–**, read as minus.

> **Note**
>
> In subtraction, the bigger number is always written on the top. That is, we always subtract the smaller number from the bigger number.
>
> | | T | O |
> |---|---|---|
> | | 5 | 6 |
> | – | 8 | 9 |
> | | | |
>
> ✗
>
> | | T | O |
> |---|---|---|
> | | 8 | 9 |
> | – | 5 | 6 |
> | | | |
>
> ✓

Terms Used in Subtraction

- **Subtrahend** is the number to be subtracted.
- **Minuend** is the greater number from which the smaller number (subtrahend) is subtracted.
- **Difference** is another word used for subtraction, which means the result obtained after subtracting two numbers.

Example: Solve 28 – 5.

	T	O
	2	8
–		5
	2	3

We have,
28 – 5 = **23**
28 is Minuend
5 is Subtrahend
23 is the difference between 28 and 5.

Subtraction Facts

1. When we subtract 0 from a number, the value of the number does not change.

   5 – 0 = **5** 98 – 0 = **98** 149 – 0 = **149**

2. When we subtract the number from itself, we get zero.

   17 – 17 = **0** 156 – 156 = **0** 183 – 183 = **0**

3. When we subtract 1 from a number, we get the number just before it.

   29 – 1 = **28** 137 – 1 = **136** 185 – 1 = **184**

> **Mental Maths**
>
> 1. 72 – 0 = ____________
> 2. 176 – 176 = ____________
> 3. 108 – 1 = ____________

SUBTRACTION WITH REGROUPING

Let us learn how to perform subtraction of

- 1-digit numbers from 2-digit numbers
- 2-digit numbers from 2-digit numbers

Subtraction of 1-Digit Numbers from 2-Digit Numbers with Regrouping

Rohit has 23 candies. Sara asked him to give her 8 candies. How many candies will be left with Rohit?

Here, we need to subtract 8 from 23, that is, 23 – 8. We write,

	T	O
	2	3
–		8

First subtract 8 from 3 in the ones column. But 8 is bigger than 3, so we cannot subtract.

	T	O
	1	13
	~~2~~	~~3~~
–		8

In this case, borrow 1 from 2 in the tens column. Then, 3 in the ones column becomes 13 and 2 in the tens column becomes 1 (since 2 – 1 = **1**). We write 13 above 8.

	T	O
	1	13
	~~2~~	~~3~~
–		8
	1	5

In the ones column, 13 – 8 = **5** and in the tens column, we are left with 1. So, 23 – 8 = **15**

Subtraction of 2-Digit Numbers from 2-Digit Numbers with Regrouping

Ajay had 25 red and green marbles. Out of them, 18 marbles were red. How many marbles were green?

Cross out 18 red marbles. We get 7 green marbles. Now, let us solve this as a subtraction problem.

		T	O
Total number of marbles =		2	5
Red marbles =	–	1	8

In the ones column 8 is greater than 5, so we cannot subtract 8 from 5. We borrow 1 from '2' in the tens column.

	T	O
	1	15
	~~2~~	~~5~~
−	1	8
		7

'2' in the tens column becomes 1 and '5' in the ones column becomes 15.

Now 15 − 8 = 7

	T	O
	1	15
	~~2~~	~~5~~
−	1	8
	0	7

Write 7 in the ones column.

Hence, there are 7 green marbles.

Common Errors

	T	O
		~~10~~
	5	0
−		3
	5	7

✗

	T	O
	4	10
	~~5~~	0
−		3
	4	7

✓

Let us see the subtraction when the greater number has 0 in the ones place.

Consider 30 − 6.

	T	O
	2	10
	~~3~~	~~0~~
−		6
	2	4

In this case, borrow 1 ten from tens place and regroup 1 ten to 10 ones.

That is, strike or cross out 0 in the ones place and write 10. Also, strike 3 in tens place and write 2.

Now, there are 2 tens and 10 ones in 30.

Take away, 6 ones from 10 ones, to get 4 ones and we are left with only 2 in the tens place. Hence, we get 24 as the answer.

EXERCISE 3A

Solve the following.

1.

	T	O
	8	5
−		7

2.

	T	O
	6	4
−	2	9

3.

	T	O
	7	3
−		5

4.

	T	O
	9	0
−	5	6

5.

	T	O
	6	4
−		8

6.

	T	O
	3	5
−	1	7

7.

	T	O
	8	0
−	4	5

8.

	T	O
	7	1
−	3	6

SUBTRACTION WITHOUT REGROUPING

Let us learn how to perform subtraction of

- 1-and 2-digit numbers from 3-digit numbers
- 3-digit numbers from 3-digit numbers

Subtraction of 1-Digit Numbers from 3-Digit Numbers

1-digit numbers are subtracted from 3-digit numbers in the same way as 1-digit numbers are subtracted from 2-digit numbers.

Common Errors

187 - 25

	H	T	O
	1	8	7
−	2	5	

×

	H	T	O
	1	8	7
−		2	5

✓

Example: Subtract 5 from 376.

Solution:

	H	T	O
	3	7	6
−			5
	3	7	1

So, 376 - 5 = 371.

Subtraction of 2-Digit Numbers from 3-Digit Numbers without regrouping

For subtracting 2-digit numbers from 3-digit numbers, first subtract the ones digits, then the tens digits and finally retain the hundred digit of the 3-digit number as it is.

Out of 145 children in class 2, 10 children were absent.

How many children were present?

Total number of children =
Number of children absent =

	H	T	O
	1	4	5
−		1	0
			5

Step 1: In the ones column, we subtract 0 from 5. We get 5 in the ones column.

	H	T	O
	1	4	5
−		1	0
		3	5

Step 1: In the tens column, we subtract 1 from 4. We get 3 in the tens column.

	H	T	O
	1	4	5
−		1	0
	1	3	5

Step 3: In the hundreds column, we have no digit to subtract from 1, hence we write, 1 in the hundreds column.

Therefore, 135 students were present.

Subtraction of 3-Digit Numbers From 3-Digit Numbers Without Regrouping

Radha bought an ice cream for ₹120. She gave ₹150 to the shopkeeper. How much money did she get in return from the shopkeeper?

We write this as a subtraction problem like,

Money given to the shopkeeper = ₹150

Cost of ice cream = ₹120

	H	T	O
Money given to shopkeeper =	1	5	0
Cost of ice cream = −	1	2	0
The shopkeeper returned ₹30 to Radha.		3	0

Note

Subtracting a number from the same numbers gives 0. If this happens in the hundreds column, we need not write 0 there.

More Examples:

1.

	H	T	O
	1	6	1
−			1
	1	6	0

2.

	H	T	O
	1	7	7
−		5	6
	1	2	1

3.

	H	T	O
	1	3	9
−		1	4
	1	2	5

4.

	H	T	O
	1	9	9
−		8	3
	1	1	6

EXERCISE 3B

Subtract the following.

1.

	H	T	O
	1	9	8
−		3	7

2.

	H	T	O
	1	4	5
−		2	0

3.

	H	T	O
	1	6	9
−	1	1	7

4.

	H	T	O
	1	7	4
−		5	3

VERIFYING SUBTRACTION USING ADDITION

A simple method to check or verify the result of subtraction using addition that works for regrouping problems as well is explained below.

A shopkeeper has 185 notebooks to sell. He sold 63 of them. Find the number of notebooks left with the shopkeeper.

We write this as,

Total number of notebooks =
Number of notebooks sold =
Number of notebooks left =

	H	T	O
	1	8	5
−		6	3
	1	2	2

He is left with 122 notebooks.

Verify

	H	T	O
	1	2	2
+		6	3
	1	8	5

The shopkeeper wishes to check if he has counted the left-over notebooks correctly.

How to verify?

The number of notebooks left (that is, the answer), if added to the number of notebooks sold should give him the total number of notebooks.

This means that the total quantity (185 here) in question should always match.

The answer must not be added to the total quantity in question. The total quantity in question must be the answer of the verification process.

EXERCISE 3C

Find the difference and verify the result using addition.

1.

	H	T	O
	1	5	4
−		2	3

Verify

	H	T	O
+			

2.

	H	T	O
	1	9	5
−	1	1	3

Verify

	H	T	O
+			

3.

	H	T	O
	1	7	8
−	1	2	3

Verify

	H	T	O
+			

4.

	H	T	O
	1	6	5
−		2	3

Verify

	H	T	O
+			

WORD PROBLEMS

We subtract when we know that the answer is going to reduce by the number given.

> **Note**
> Look out for subtraction words in a problem. Words like:
> Subtract, difference, minus, take away, deduct, decrease, less than, reduce by, how many were left, how many more, by how much, etc.

Examples:

1. 24 less than 156 is written as,

	H	T	O
	1	5	6
–		2	4
	1	3	2

In the ones column, 6 – 4 = **2**

In the tens column, 5 – 2 = **3**

In the hundreds column, there is nothing to subtract so, we write 1 as it is.

156 – 24 = **132**

2. Take away 47 from 93. This is written as,

	T	O
	9	3
–	4	7

	T	O
	8	13
	~~9~~	~~3~~
–	4	7
	4	6

93 - 47 = **46**

> **Go Easy!**
> The number written after the word 'from' is the bigger number and must be kept on top while subtracting.

3. Monu weighs 56 kg. Sonu weighs 13 kg less than Monu. How much does Sonu weigh?

Solution: Monu weighs
Sonu would weigh less by

	T	O
	5	6
–	1	3
	4	3

Therefore, Sonu weighs 43 kg.

4. Banrap bought 85 mango ice creams for some guests at home. 29 ice creams melted on his way. How many ice creams were still ready to be eaten?

Solution:

Total number of ice creams =
Number of melted ice creams =

	T	O
	7	15
	~~8~~	~~5~~
–	2	9
	5	6

So, 56 ice creams were still ready to be eaten.

EXERCISE 3D

Solve the following and verify by using addition.

1. 38 less than 159 is

	H	T	O
	1	5	9
−		3	8

Verify

	H	T	O
+			

2. Take away 77 from 178

	H	T	O
	1	7	8
−		7	7

Verify

	H	T	O
+			

3. Out of 76 toffees, the teacher distributed 54 toffees, how many toffees were left?
4. There were 93 cars parked in the car parking area. 48 of them were blue cars and the rest were all red cars. How many red cars were there?

5. Out of 165 roses at the florist's shop, 54 roses were red. The rest of the roses were pink. How many roses were pink?

6. In a school, there were 156 chairs and 41 tables. How many more chairs were there than tables?

Mental Maths

1. Out of the numbers given choose different pairs of numbers whose difference is 10.

10 29 55 52 62 39 45 20

2. Take out 4 tens from 80 ______________.
3. 187 is 1 less than ______________.
4. a. 10 subtracted from 110 gives ________________.

   b. 50 subtracted from the above result gives ________________.

PUZZLE!

The teacher of class 2 announced the marks obtained by students in a Maths test in the form of a puzzle.
She said that,

1. Anil got 95 – 12 = ____________ marks in the test.
2. Sumit got 18 marks less than 118 = ____________ in the test.
3. Sid got 10 marks less than Anil's marks. He got ____________.
4. If you take away 28 from 123, you will get the marks that Ameeta got. She got ____________ marks.
5. Sanah got Ameeta's marks reduced by 35. She got ____________ marks.

Do you know?

The method of subtraction, that is, **borrowing**, originated somewhere around the year 1200. The word borrow, was not commonly used until around the year 1600. It was discovered when there was a situation to take 6 out of nothing, that is zero.

Maths Lab Activity

Aim: To understand the concept of subtracting two 2-digit numbers

Materials required: Playing cards, a notebook, a pencil

Procedure: 1. Make two teams of the students in your class. Let each team have a set of playing cards. Take out the Jack, Queen and the King of each set. Let each team take out 2 cards to make get two 2-digit numbers.

2. Both the teams should now find out the difference between these two 2-digit numbers. The team that finds out faster wins.

1 6 8 2

	T	O
	7	12
	~~8~~	~~2~~
–	1	6
	6	6

82 – 16 = **66**

Since 82 is bigger, we subtract 16 from 82.

Conclusion: This will help students to learn subtraction of 2-digit numbers with regrouping faster.

Concept Map

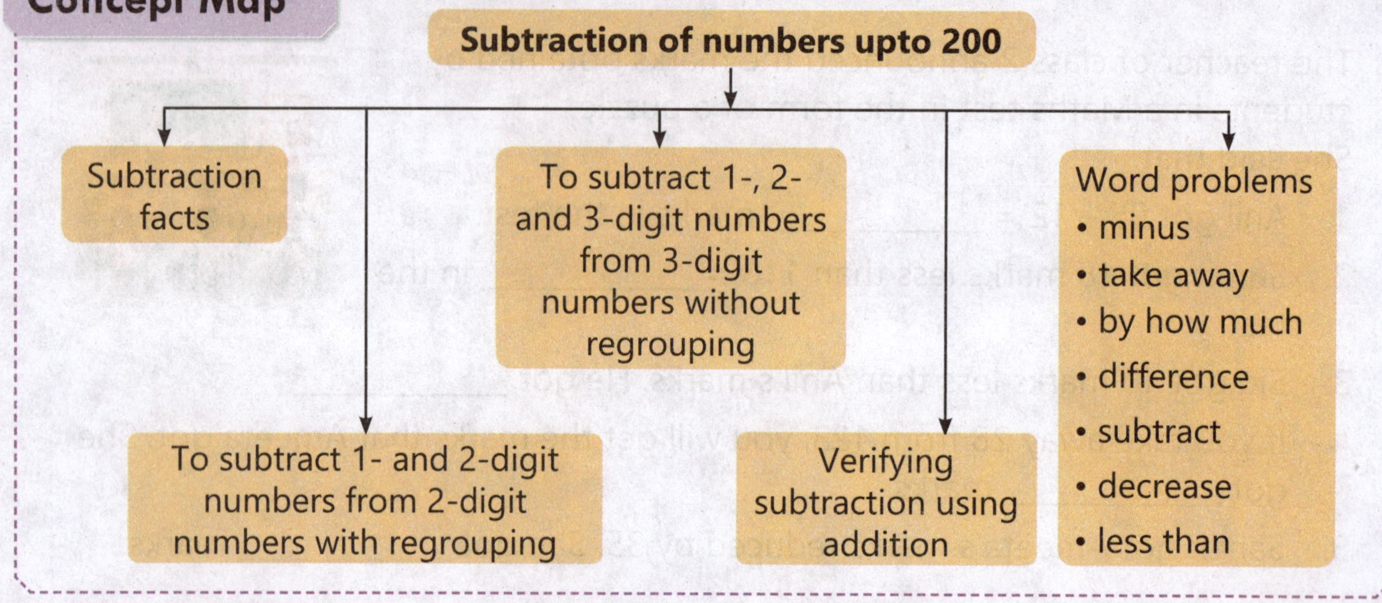

Key Concepts

- **Subtraction:** The process of taking away one number from another number. If the value of a quantity or a number decreases, we subtract.
- **Difference:** Another word used for subtraction, which means the **result** obtained after subtracting two numbers.
- **Subtraction words:** Subtract, difference, minus, take away, deduct, decrease, less than, reduce by, how many were left, how many more, by how much, etc.
- **Regrouping in subtraction**: When we cannot subtract a bigger number from a smaller number, we should borrow 1 tens and add it to the number in the ones value. 1 tens = 10 ones. This concept is called **regrouping** in subtraction.
- **Subtrahend:** The number to be subtracted
- **Minuend:** The greater number from which the smaller number (subtrahend) is subtracted
- **Subtraction facts:** Rules of subtraction
  - ➢ When we subtract 0 from a number, the value of the number does not change.
  - ➢ When we subtract the number from itself, we get zero.
  - ➢ When we subtract 1 from a number, we get the number just before it.
- We learnt,
  - ➢ subtraction of 1- and 2-digit numbers with regrouping
  - ➢ subtraction of 1-, 2- and 3-digit numbers from 3-digit numbers without regrouping
- While verifying a subtraction problem, the total quantity in question must be the answer of the verification process.

Chapter Revision

A. Solve the following.

1.

	H	T	O
	1	4	7
–		1	1

2.

	H	T	O
	1	6	9
–		2	8

3.

	H	T	O
	1	6	5
–		1	5

4.

	H	T	O
	1	3	4
–		2	0

B. Subtract the following.

	T	O
	7	4
–	2	9

Circle all the numbers that are greater than the answer.

12 174 89 31 62 158 6 9 44 180

C. Match the following.

Column A **Column B**

1.

	T	O
	7	4
–	2	0

113

2.

	H	T	O
	1	3	8
–		2	5

36

3.

	T	O
	9	2
–	5	6

142

4.

	H	T	O
	1	8	9
–		4	7

54

D. Subtract and verify.

1.

	H	T	O
	1	5	4
−		2	3

Verify

	H	T	O
+			

2.

	H	T	O
	1	9	5
−	1	1	3

Verify

	H	T	O
+			

E. Write T for true and F for false.

1. We must subtract the bigger number from the smaller number always. ☐
2. If we subtract a number from itself, we get 1. ☐
3. 10 less than 190 is 200. ☐
4. 23 taken away from 155 is 132. ☐

F. Fill in the blanks.

1. There are 98 – 10 = ________________ children in class 2.
2. Sachin wanted to give each child a chocolate.

He brought 84 – 12 = ________________ chocolates.

He needs ________________ more chocolates.

G. Answer the following.

1. Sarobara bought 199 balloons.
   a. She put up 51 balloons for her birthday party. How many balloons was she left with?
   b. She hung 6 balloons around her birthday cake. How many balloons was she left with now?

2. Out of 175 monkeys in a zoo, 22 monkeys ran away. How many monkeys were left in the zoo?

3. Out of 176 children in a school, 52 children came by car. The rest of the children came in the school bus. How many children came in the school bus?

SKILL UP!

Project

Make two teams. Give each team two dice to roll. When each team rolls the two dice, we get a 2-digit number. Tell them to form two 2-digit numbers alternatively each time and then find the difference between them.

Life Skills

34 children were running in a race competition. Out of them, Ameer fell and hurt himself. Two other participants, Sumit and Rajdeep stopped and helped Ameer to get up and took him to the side of the racing track.

How many children could complete the race? ____________

Have you ever participated in a racing competition? ____________

Have you ever helped someone in need? Which is more important, winning or participating? ______________________________

Mind Buzzer

Consider the proverb.

'The grass is always greener on the other side of the fence'

Write down all the vowels and the consonants. Count them and find the difference between the number of vowels and the number of consonants.

Hint: There are 26 letters in the English alphabet. The letters a, e, i, o and u are called vowels. The other letters are called consonants.

Teacher's Notes

- Children must understand that subtraction means taking away.
- Subtracting with regrouping becomes easier if we can explain it to the children using balls or sticks. Each stick can become tens and each ball can become ones. Explain to the children that by borrowing one stick, we get ten balls.

WORKSHEET

Solve the subtraction problems. Use the colour codes to colour the picture.

Hint: **The background of the picture is light green in colour.**

Colour Codes

56 = Light green
42 = Yellow
68 = Orange
66 = Blue

n. $79 - 23 = \_\_\_$

a. $88 - 20 = \_\_\_$

b. $90 - 48 = \_\_\_$

o. $92 - 36 = \_\_\_$

l. $80 - 38 = \_\_\_$

c. $90 - 22 = \_\_\_$

k. $188 - 120 = \_\_\_$

d. $92 - 50 = \_\_\_$

m. $90 - 24 = \_\_\_$

j. $71 - 29 = \_\_\_$

e. $199 - 131 = \_\_\_$

i. $79 - 11 = \_\_\_$

f. $182 - 140 = \_\_\_$

h. $89 - 47 = \_\_\_$

g. $89 - 21 = \_\_\_$

p. $198 - 142 = \_\_\_$

q. $80 - 24 = \_\_\_$

4 Numbers up to 1000

Learning Objectives

- To learn about 3-digit numbers and represent them on the number line
- To learn the place value, face value and expanded form
- To compare 3-digit numbers
- To learn ascending and descending orders of 3-digit numbers
- To learn numbers before, after and in between other numbers

Let's Get Started

Given below are pictures of Ameeta's family with their ages.

1. Write the number names of Ameeta's:
   a. Father's age ________________ b. Mother's age ________________
2. Find Ameeta's grandfather's age, if he is three years older than Ameeta's grandmother.
   (in numerals) ____
   (in words) ____

3. Write Ameeta's friend's age, if she is one year younger than Ameeta. (in words) ____________________________________
4. Arrange the age of each member in ascending order.
   ____
5. Fill in the blanks.
   a. 83 = ______ tens ______ ones b. 97 = ______ tens ______ ones
   c. In 64, place value of 6 is ______ and face value of 6 is ______.

INTRODUCTION TO 3-DIGIT NUMBERS

Rohit has 99 colourful marbles. He found one more marble. How many marbles does he have now?

Adding 1 marble to 99 marbles, we have,

	H	T	O
		9	9
+			1
	1	0	0

Hundreds	Tens	Ones
1	0	0

Do you know?

A 100 year makes a century.

When you score 100 runs in Cricket, it is also known as a century.

It introduces the place value of **hundreds** after ones and tens.

The **number name** for 100 is **one hundred**.

100 can be represented by the block shown below.

Note

100 is the smallest 3-digit number.

This block has one hundred squares. There are 10 squares in each row and in each column.

	Numeral	Number Name
	100	One hundred
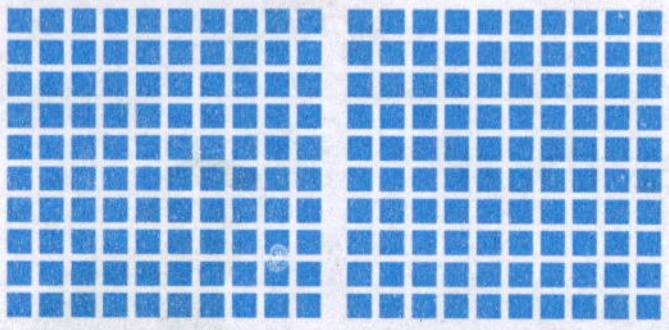	200	Two hundred
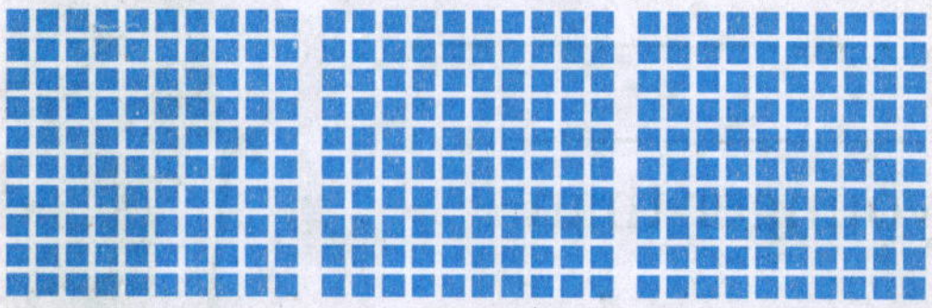	300	Three hundred
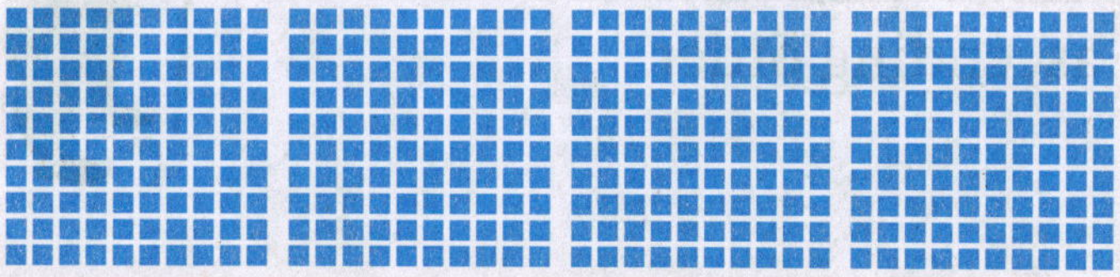	400	Four hundred

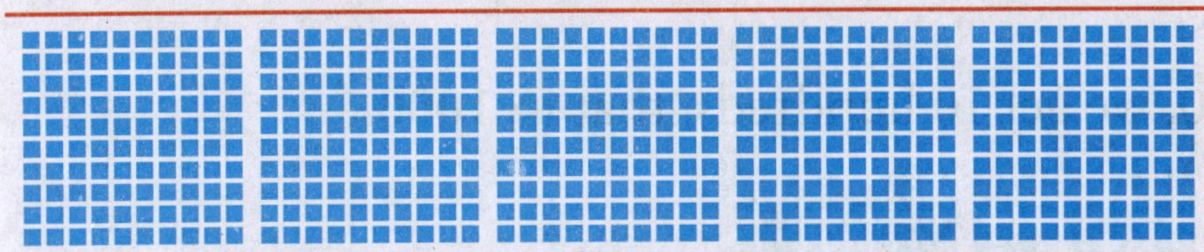	500	Five hundred
	600	Six hundred
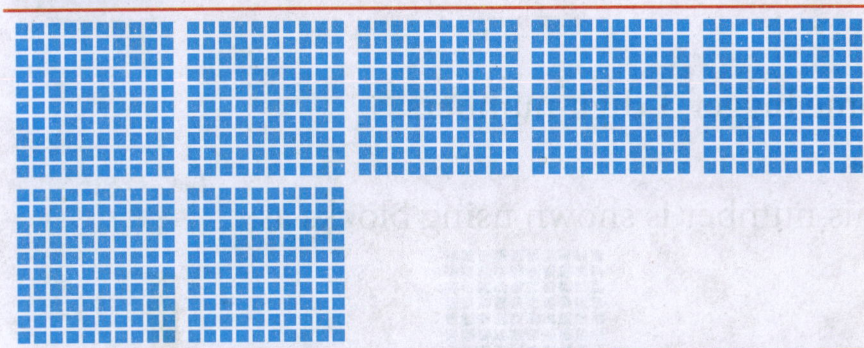	700	Seven hundred
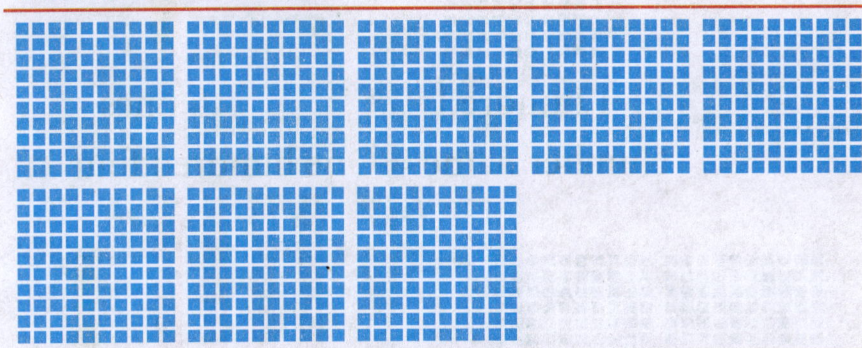	800	Eight hundred
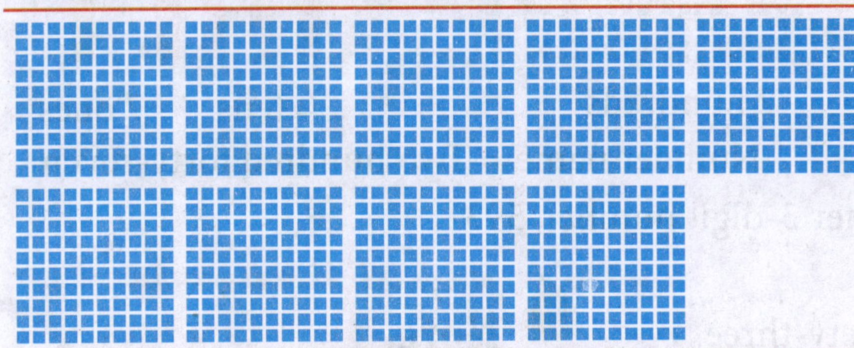	900	Nine hundred

The Number 1000

By combining ten blocks of 100, we get 10 hundreds, that is, **1000**.

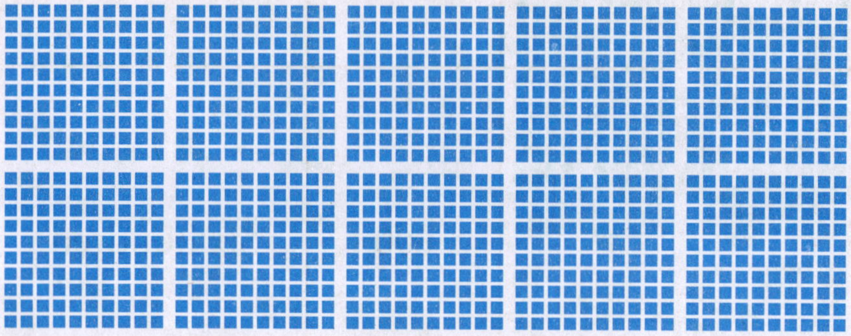

1000 One thousand

> **Note**
> 1000 is the smallest 4-digit number.

1000 is read as **one thousand**.

More 3-digit Numbers

Let us learn and understand some bigger 3-digit numbers.

Consider a 3-digit number, 104.

We can write it as

Hundreds	Tens	Ones
1	0	4

This number is shown using blocks as:

1 hundred 4 ones

Number name = One hundred four

Consider another example.

The number, 247.

Hundreds	Tens	Ones
2	4	7

2 hundreds 4 tens 7 ones

Number name = Two hundred forty-seven

Let us now have a look at another 3-digit number, 593.

How do we read 593?

593 is read as five hundred ninety-three.

H	T	O
5	9	3
↓	↓	↓
Five hundred	ninety	three

> **Note**
> The last two digits of a 3-digit number are read together.
> **Examples:**
> 4<u>72</u> = Four hundred <u>seventy-two</u>
> 3<u>99</u> = Three hundred <u>ninety-nine</u>

EXERCISE 4A

1. Fill in the blanks.

a. 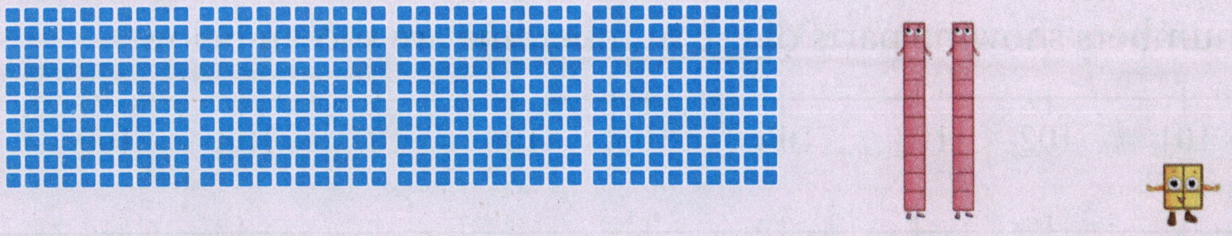

____ hundreds ____ tens ____ ones

Number name = ______________________________

b. 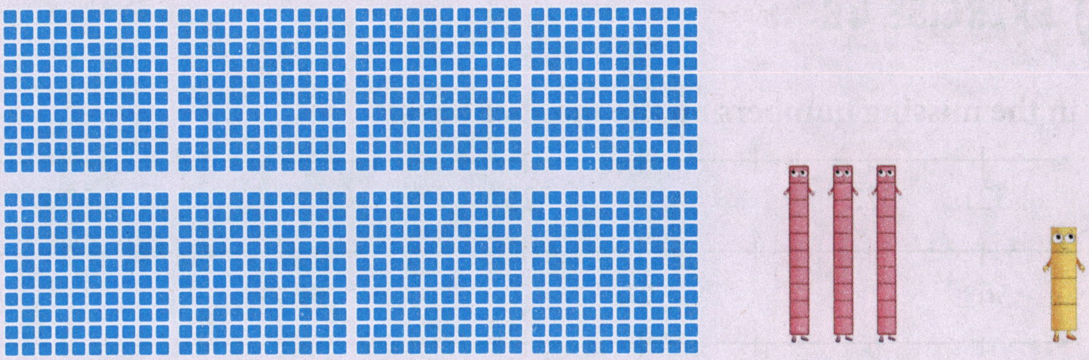

____ hundreds ____ tens ____ ones

Number name = ______________________________

2. Fill in the blanks.

a. 906 = ________ hundreds ________ tens ________ ones

Number name = ______________________________

b. 243 = ________ hundreds ________ tens ________ ones

Number name = ______________________________

3. Write the numerals.

a. Four hundred thirty-one ________ b. Nine hundred sixty-three ________

c. Six hundred nineteen ________ d. Eight hundred seventy-one ________

4. Encircle the number that comes just after the numbers given below.

a. 472 – 192 587 690 473

b. 861 – 793 862 258 720

5. Write three numbers that come after the following numbers.

a. 362, ______, ______, ______ b. 574, ______, ______, ______

c. 193, ______, ______, ______ d. 845, ______, ______, ______

REPRESENTATION OF 3-DIGIT NUMBERS ON NUMBER LINE

The **number line** is a line which shows the order of numbers as we count them. The number line is extended by adding 1 every time. To get to the next number, we increase the digit in the ones place by 1.

Some numbers showing parts of the number line are shown below.

10<u>1</u> 10<u>2</u> 10<u>3</u> 10<u>4</u> 10<u>5</u> 10<u>6</u> 10<u>7</u> 10<u>8</u> 10<u>9</u> 11<u>0</u>

51<u>1</u> 51<u>2</u> 51<u>3</u> 51<u>4</u> 51<u>5</u> 51<u>6</u> 51<u>7</u> 51<u>8</u> 51<u>9</u> 52<u>0</u>

EXERCISE 4B

Fill in the missing numbers on the number lines.

1. 321, 322, ___, ___, 325, ___, ___, ___, 329, 330
2. 541, ___, ___, 544, ___, ___, 547, ___, ___, 550
3. 831, ___, ___, ___, 835, ___, ___, 838, ___, ___
4. 671, ___, ___, ___, 675, ___, ___, 678, ___, 680

PLACE VALUE AND FACE VALUE

Place Value: In numbers, each digit is assigned a value. It is referred to as its place value.

Let us learn about the place value of 3-digit numbers.

Note

To write the place value of a number, write the number followed by as many zeros as there are digits to the right of the number.

Examples: Consider the following numbers.

1. 539

H	T	O
5	3	9

The place value of 5 is 500.
The place value of 3 is 30.
The place value of 9 is 9.

2. 721

H	T	O
7	2	1

The place value of 7 is 700.
The place value of 2 is 20.
The place value of 1 is 1.

Face Value: The face value of a number is the number itself.

Examples: Consider the numbers, 539 and 721.

H	T	O
5	3	9

The face value of 5 is 5.
The face value of 3 is 3.
The face value of 9 is 9.

H	T	O
7	2	1

The face value of 7 is 7.
The face value of 2 is 2.
The face value of 1 is 1.

EXPANDED FORM OF 3-DIGIT NUMBERS

Consider the following examples to learn expanded form of 3-digit numbers.

Example 1: Write the expanded form of 258.

H	T	O
2	5	8

= 2 hundreds 5 tens 8 ones
or 258 = 200 + 50 + 8

Example 2: Write the expanded form of 973.

H	T	O
9	7	3

= 9 hundreds 7 tens 3 ones
or 973 = 900 + 70 + 3

Note

If the expanded form of a number is 200 + 90 + 9, then the short form is 299.
Example: Short form of 800 + 70 + 3 is 873.

Common Errors

Expanded form of 349

349 = 3 + 4 + 9 ✗

349 = 300 + 40 + 9 ✓

EXERCISE 4C

1. Write the place values and the face values.

a. 173

Place value of	Face value of
1 = ______	1 = ______
7 = ______	7 = ______
3 = ______	3 = ______

b. 684

Place value of	Face value of
6 = ______	6 = ______
8 = ______	8 = ______
4 = ______	4 = ______

2. Write in expanded form.

a. 385 = ______ hundreds ______ tens ______ ones

OR

385 = ______ + ______ + ______

b. 691 = ______ hundreds ______ tens ______ ones

OR

691 = ______ + ______ + ______

3. **Write the place value of the underlined digits of the numbers.**

a. $\underline{3}81$ ____ b. $4\underline{7}6$ ____ c. $59\underline{2}$ ____

4. **Write the face value of the underlined digits of the numbers.**

a. $1\underline{4}8$ ____ b. $\underline{9}37$ ____ c. $25\underline{6}$ ____

5. **Fill in the blanks.**

a. Short form of 500 + 30 + 2 = ____________

b. Face value of 7 in 107 = ____________

c. Place value of 4 in 849 = ____________

d. Expanded form of 909 = ____________

COMPARING NUMBERS

Let us compare and find:

- greater or lesser of the two numbers
- greatest or smallest among more than two numbers
- **When the number of digits is different.**

Which number is greater?

T	O
6	3

OR

H	T	O
1	5	8

63 is a 2-digit number

158 is a 3-digit number

158 > 63

Note

Out of the two numbers being compared, the number with more number of digits is always the greater number.

Common Errors

99 > 300 ✗ 99 < 300 ✓

99 starts with a 9 and 300 starts with a 3

But 300 is bigger, because it is a 3–digit number.

99 is a 2–digit number.

- **When the number of digits is same.**

a.

H	T	O
$\underline{4}$	6	7

OR

H	T	O
$\underline{9}$	3	5

Check the digits placed at the hundreds place in both the numbers and compare.

We know that 9 is greater than 4. Therefore, 467 < 935.

b.

H	T	O
6	7	3

OR

H	T	O
6	2	4

The digits placed at the hundreds place are same, that is, 6.

Now, check the digits placed at the tens place in both the numbers and compare. 7 is greater than 2. Therefore, 673 [>] 624.

c.

H	T	O
1	2	5

OR

H	T	O
1	2	6

H	T	O
1	2	5

H	T	O
1	2	6

Here we find that the digits at the hundreds place in both the numbers are 1.

H	T	O
1	2	5

H	T	O
1	2	6

Here we find that the digits at the tens place in both the numbers are 2.

H	T	O
1	2	5

H	T	O
1	2	6

The digits at the ones place in both the numbers are 5 and 6. 6 is bigger than 5. Therefore, 125 [<] 126.

- **When all the three digits are same and placed in the same way, then both the numbers are equal.**

H	T	O
9	6	7

or

H	T	O
9	6	7

The digits at the hundreds place, tens place and ones place in both the numbers are same. They are 9, 6 and 7 respectively.

Therefore, 967 [=] 967.

EXERCISE 4D

1. **Compare the numbers and put the correct sign (>, < or =).**

   a. 964 [ ] 182 b. 729 [ ] 607 c. 200 [ ] 800

   d. 521 [ ] 906 e. 374 [ ] 374 f. 189 [ ] 183

2. **Encircle the greatest number in each set of numbers.**

   a. 237, 569, 481 b. 729, 843, 669 c. 485, 127, 489

3. **Encircle the smallest number in each set of numbers.**

   a. 478, 926, 650 b. 769, 238, 815 c. 347, 529, 341

ORDERING OF NUMBERS

Ascending order of numbers means **numbers in an increasing order.**

Example: 156, 204, 739, 845

Ascending order means arranging from smallest to greatest.

Descending order of numbers means **numbers in a decreasing order.**

Example: 973, 805, 612, 497

Descending order means arranging from greatest to smallest.

Example 1: Arrange the numbers in ascending order.

629, 173, 805, 467

Solution:

Step 1: Check the digits placed at the hundreds place of all the numbers. The number with the smallest digit in the hundreds place is the smallest number.

Step 2: The next greater digit placed at the hundreds place is the next number and so on.

The order of the numbers is marked as given below.

629,	173,	805,	467
3	1	4	2

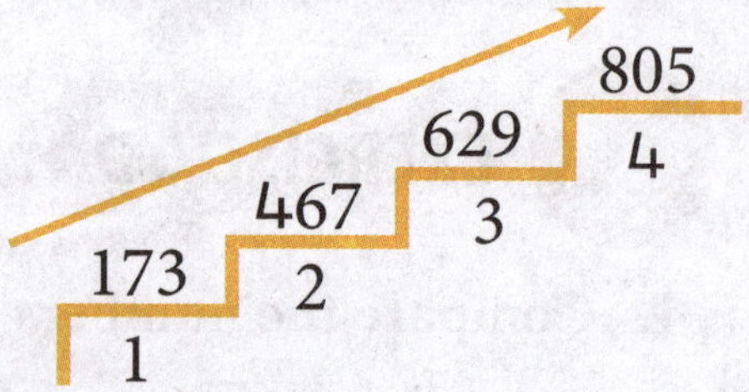

Hence, the ascending order of these numbers is:

173, 467, 629, 805

Example 2: Arrange the numbers in descending order.

295, 876, 531, 408

Solution:

Step 1: Check the digits placed at the hundreds place of all the numbers. The number with the greatest digit placed at the hundreds place is the greatest number.

Step 2: The next smaller digit at the hundreds place is the next number and so on.

The order of the numbers is marked as given below.

295,	876,	531,	408
4	1	2	3

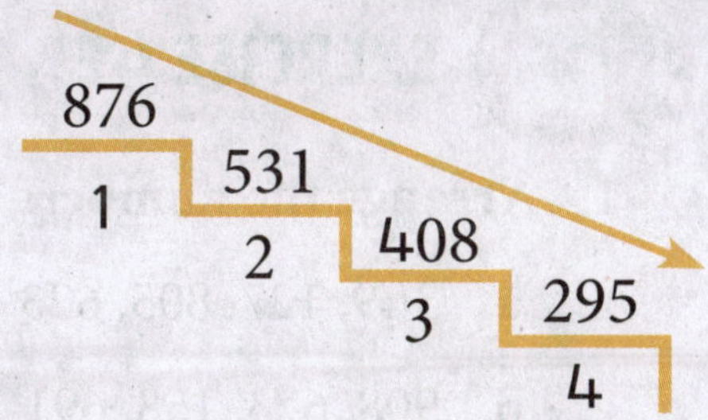

Hence, the descending order of these numbers is:

876, 531, 408, 295

Ordering Numbers in 10s

Let us now count numbers in periods of 10. In this case, we skip 10 numbers every time. That means, there is a gap of 10 numbers between any two numbers. Following numbers have been arranged in periods of 10 in ascending order.

Complete the patterns.

a. 120, 130, 140, 150, 160, 170, ______, ______ ______, ______, ______

b. 310, 320, 330, 340, 350, 360, ______, ______ ______, ______, ______

c. 550, 560, 570, 580, 590, 600, ______, ______ ______, ______, ______

d. 780, 790, 800, 810, 820, 830, ______, ______ ______, ______, ______

Following numbers have been arranged in periods of 10 in descending order.

Complete the patterns.

a. 490, 480, 470, 460, 450, 440, ______, ______ ______, ______, ______

b. 580, 570, 560, 550, 540, 530, ______, ______ ______, ______, ______

c. 850, 840, 830, 820, 810, 800, ______, ______ ______, ______, ______

d. 930, 920, 910, 900, 890, 880, ______, ______ ______, ______, ______

We can also arrange numbers in ascending or descending order in periods of 100. For ascending order, add 1 to the digit in the hundreds position. For descending order, subtract 1 from the digit in the hundreds position.

EXERCISE 4E

1. **Arrange the numbers in ascending order.**
   a. 349, 127, 805, 623 ________, ________, ________, ________
   b. 908, 673, 158, 691 ________, ________, ________, ________
2. **Arrange the numbers in descending order.**
   a. 573, 189, 640, 257 ________, ________, ________, ________
   b. 329, 746, 150, 928 ________, ________, ________, ________
3. **Complete the patterns.**
   a. 540, 550, ________, ________, ________, ________
   b. 376, 476, ________, ________, ________, ________
   c. 780, 770, ________, ________, ________, ________
   d. 940, 930, ________, ________, ________, ________

BEFORE, AFTER, IN-BETWEEN

Let us understand the differences between

- before and just before
- after and just after

Sam and his friends are standing in a line.

1. Radhika is standing **just before** Sam.

   Nick, Khilee, Kavya and Radhika are standing **before** Sam.

   Now consider the following sequence of numbers.

   125, 126, 127, 128, 129, 130

   129 comes **just before** 130 and 125, 126, 127, 128, 129 come **before** 130.

Note

To find the number just before, subtract 1 from the digit in the ones position.

To find the number just after, add 1 to the digit in the ones position.

2. Khilee is standing **just after** Nick.

Khilee, Kavya, Radhika and Sam are standing **after** Nick.

Hence, in the sequence of numbers given below,

125, 126, 127, 128, 129, 130

126 comes **just after** 125 and 126, 127, 128, 129, 130 come **after** 125.

Let us practise a few problems.

Example 1: Write the number that comes just before 468.

a. ______, 468

467, 468

Example 2: Write the number that comes just after.

b. 333, ______

333, 334

Example 3: Write the numbers that come in between the given numbers.

a. 394, ______, 396

394, 395, 396

b. 721, ______, ______, 724

721, 722, 723, 724

EXERCISE 4F

1. **Write the number that comes just after the given number.**

   a. 135, ______ b. 623, ______ c. 467, ______ d. 854, ______

2. **Write the number that comes just before the given number.**

   a. ______, 275 b. ______, 498 c. ______, 614 d. ______, 801

3. **Write the numbers that come in between the given numbers.**

   a. 234, ______, 236 b. 721, ______, 723

   c. 946, ______, 948 d. 669, ______, ______, 672

4. **Write two numbers that come after 445.** ______________

5. **Write three numbers that come before 871.** ______________

FORMATION OF NUMBERS

Numbers can be formed by arranging the given digits in ascending order or descending order.

Example 1: Arrange the digits 5 and 6 to form the greatest number and the smallest number.

The greatest number formed using the digits 5 and 6 is 65.

The smallest number formed using the digits 5 and 6 is 56.

Example 2: Arrange the digits 5, 0 and 7 to form the greatest number and the smallest number.

The greatest number formed using the digits 5, 0 and 7 is 750.

The smallest number formed using the digits 5, 0 and 7 is 507.

EXERCISE 4G

Arrange the following digits to form the greatest and the smallest numbers.

	Digits	Greatest Number	Smallest Number
1.	3 and 8	________	________
2.	1 and 5	________	________
3.	2, 0 and 9	________	________
4.	4, 6 and 7	________	________

Go Easy!

Formation of numbers with 0 as one of the digits

- If 0 is one of the digits in a 3-digit number, do not place it at the hundreds position. In that case, always place 0 at the tens position. If 0 is placed at the hundreds position, it then becomes a 2-digit number.
- Similarly, to form a 2-digit number, do not place 0 at the tens position. Always place it at the ones position. Otherwise, it will become a 1-digit number.

CROSSWORD

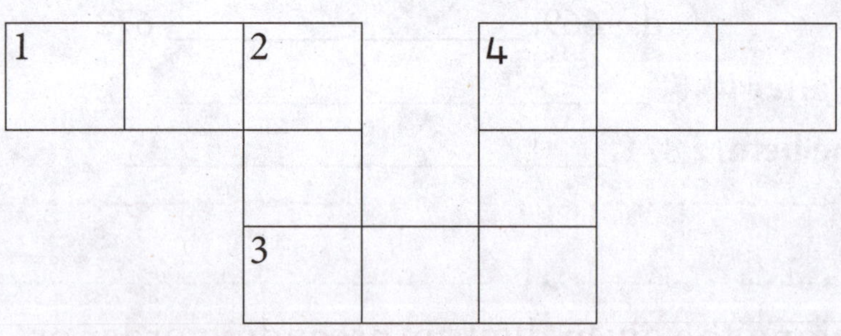

Across

1. I am 1 more than 627.
3. I am 10 more than 572.
4. I am 100 less than 891.

Down

2. I have 5 in the ones position and 9 in the tens position.
4. I have 7 in the hundreds position and 3 in the tens position.

Mental Maths

1. ________ is the smallest 4-digit number. Write its number name. ____________________.
2. ________ is the place value of 6 in 536. What is the face value of 3? ________
3. Place value and face value of a digit are same when the digit is placed at the ________ position.
4. Expanded form of 391 is ________.
5. Use >, < or =. 459 ________ 495.
6. The greatest number formed using 8, 0 and 9 is _______.

Maths Lab Activity

Aim: To find the smallest number out of a given set of numbers

Materials required: Notebook, pen, number plates of cars

Procedure:

1. Take a walk in your locality with a notebook and a pen and observe the number plates of 10 cars.
2. Now, note down the last three digits of all the numbers on the number plates of these cars. Write these numbers in an ascending order.
3. Which is the smallest number out of these numbers?

Conclusion: We learnt how different 3-digit numbers can be compared in real life.

Concept Map

Numbers up to 1000

- 3-digit numbers on the number line
- Place value and face value
- Expanded form of 3-digit numbers
- Comparing 3-digit numbers
- Ascending order and descending order
- Formation of numbers

Key Concepts

- Numbers up to 1000 can be represented on the number line.
- **Ordering numbers in 10s:** We can arrange the numbers with periods of 10 in ascending or descending order.
- Numbers can be formed by arranging them in different orders.

Chapter Revision

A. Fill in the blanks.

1. 

____ hundreds ____ tens ____ ones

Number name = ____________________

2. 

____ hundreds ____ tens ____ ones

Number name = ____________________

3. ____________________ is the greatest 3-digit number.
4. The short form of 600 + 50 + 3 is ____________________.
5. The greatest number formed using the digits 3, 9 and 0 is ____________________.
6. The ascending order for 821, 811, 819, 919, 812 is ____________________.

B. Write the missing numbers on the number line given below.

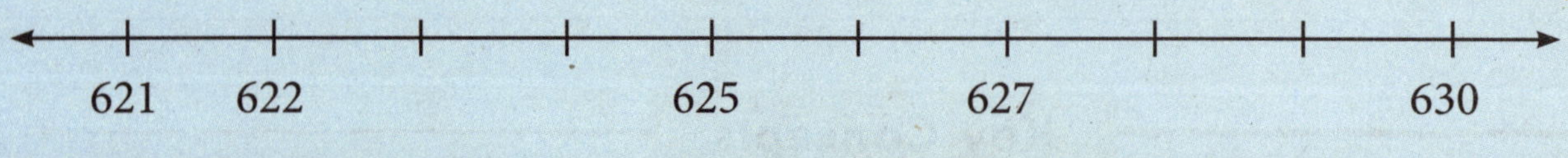

C. The students decorated the school premises with 125 balloons at the school fete.

1. Write the number name of 125. ____________________
2. Write the expanded form of 125. ____________________
3. Write the place value and face value of 2 in 125. ____________________

D. Write T for true and F for false.

1. 771 is greater than 779. ☐
2. 421 is the smallest 3-digit number formed using the digits 1, 2 and 4. ☐
3. The numeral for five hundred twenty-nine is 529. ☐
4. The face value of 8 in 180 is 80. ☐
5. The numbers 391, 310, 317, 371 are in descending order. ☐

E. Compare the numbers and put the correct sign (>, < or =).

a. 431 ☐ 485 b. 221 ☐ 212

c. 398 ☐ 432 d. 817 ☐ 877

F. Complete the patterns.

1. 510, 610, ________, ________, ________

2. 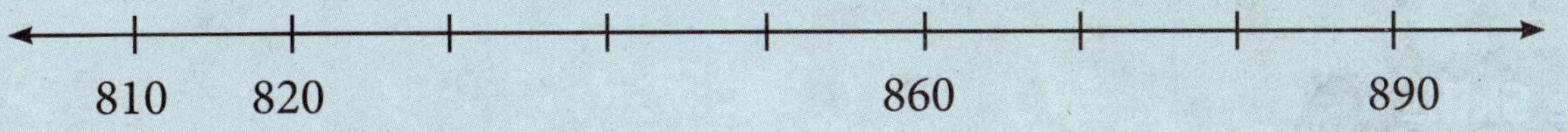

G. Write the number that comes just after 455. ________

H. Write four numbers that come after 237 ________, ________, ________ **and** ________.

I. Write any four numbers that come in between 984 and 999.

________, ________, ________ **and** ________.

J. Write the short form of 200 + 10 + 1. Write its number name.

____

SKILL UP!

Project

1. Few children can cut cards and write 100 on 9 cards and 10 on 9 more cards. They should also write digits from 1 to 9 on another set of 9 cards. Now, they can ask each other to form numbers like 453, 129, 390, 800, etc. To form 453, we can use cards as given below.

100	100	100	100	10	10	10	10	10	3

   To form 129, we can use cards as given below.

100	10	10	9

   Ask them to call aloud the number names of the numbers as well.
2. Find the heights of some of the tallest buildings in the world. The heights should be 3-digit numbers.
   (**Example:** height of World Trade Center in New York, U.S.A. is 417 m)

Life Skills

There were floods in a village where 400 people lived. The government provided packets of food and water bottles for the villagers. Tick (✓) the correct estimate.

a. How many packets of food should they provide? 8, 80, 800
b. How many bottles of water should they lend? 9, 90, 900

How do you help the poor people? State your experience briefly.

Mind Buzzer

Guess who I am?

I'm a 3-digit number. I have 7 in my ones place. I have 5 in my tens place.

The digit at my hundreds place has 900 as the place value.

I am ____________________

Teacher's Notes

- Let the students collect a set of 100 similar types of buttons and make a grid of 10 × 10 on a table, they will understand the quantity of 100 in a better way. They can make 2 to 3 such grids to understand the quantity of 200 and 300 as well.
- Make them form numbers with the help of flash cards (with different digits on them).
- Writing numbers from 1 to 1000 will give them practice in number formation. Calling aloud the number names of numbers will help them learn the number names faster.

WORKSHEET

A fruit seller had the following quantity of fruits to sell in his shop.

670

680

780

920

1. Write the number names of the quantity of all the fruits in the shop.

   a. Apple ____________________

   b. Bananas ____________________

   c. Grapes ____________________

   d. Strawberries ____________________

2. Write the place value of all the digits in the quantity of grapes.

Digits	Place value
7	________
8	________
0	________

3. Which fruit was 10 more than apples in quantity? ____________

4. Which fruit was 100 less than grapes in quantity? ____________

5. The quantity of which fruit is the greatest? ____________

6. The quantity of which fruit is the least? ____________

7. Write the names of the fruits in their descending order, in terms of quantity.

   ____

5 Addition of Bigger Numbers

Learning Objectives

- To add bigger 2-digit numbers with regrouping
- To learn addition of 2-digit and 3-digit numbers without regrouping
- To learn addition of 3-digit numbers without regrouping
- To learn about correct placement of numbers while adding.
- To solve word problems involving addition of bigger numbers

Let's Get Started

John and Meg went to a school fete with their parents. There were swings, food joints, games, fun activities, etc. Solve the sums given below and find your answers in the fete scene given. Draw lines. One is done for you.

A

	T	O
	2	4
+	3	3
	5	7

B

	T	O
	4	9
+	1	2

C

	T	O
	6	1
+	3	6

D

	T	O
	9	8
+		1

E

	T	O
	2	5
	1	3
+	2	2

F

	T	O
	3	3
	2	1
+	1	8

G

	T	O
	1	1
	2	3
+	3	4

H

	T	O
	1	0
	1	1
+	4	9

How many numbers could you find? ____________.

ADDING BIGGER 2-DIGIT NUMBERS WITH REGROUPING

We have learnt about adding three 2-digit numbers in previous classes. Let us take some bigger 2-digit numbers and add them.

> **Note**
> Adding bigger 2-digit numbers results in 3-digit numbers.

Regrouping from Ones to Tens

Example 1: 88 + 74

When we add 88 and 74, we place them as shown below.

Solution:

	H	T	O
		8	8
+		7	4

Step 1:
First add the numbers in the ones column, that is, 8 + 4 = **12**

	H	T	O
		1	
		8	8
+		7	4
			2

Step 2:
Write '2' of 12 in the ones column. Carry forward '1' of 12. Write it above 8 in the tens column.

	H	T	O
		1	
		8	8
+		7	4
	1	6	2

Step 3:
Solve 1 + 8 + 7 given in the tens column. We get 16. Write 1 of 16 in hundreds column and 6 of 16 in the tens column.

So, 88 + 74 = **162**

Let us consider the case when adding the tens digits results in a 2-digit number.

Example 2: Denny wants to distribute 55 sweets on his birthday and Rex wants to distribute 89 sweets. Find the total number of sweets that they want to distribute.

Solution: We will find the total number of sweets as shown below.

	H	T	O
		1	
		5	5
+		8	9
	1	4	4

Solve 5 + 9 given in the ones column. We get 14.
Carry forward 1 to tens column. Write 1 above 5.
Write 4 in the ones column. Solve 1 + 5 + 8. We get 14.
Write 4 of 14 in tens column and 1 of 14 in hundreds column.
So, 55 + 89 = **144**

EXERCISE 5A

1. **Add the following.**

a.

	H	T	O
		5	8
+		7	1

b.

	H	T	O
		2	6
+		9	4

c.

	H	T	O
		7	4
+		3	7

d.

	H	T	O
		6	7
+		5	8

2. **Aman has 66 coins and Raman has 55 coins. What is the total number of coins with them?**

	H	T	O
+			

3. **Kelly has 87 flowers in her garden. She plans to have 50 more flowers. Find the total number of flowers Kelly plans to have.**

	H	T	O
+			

ADDING 2-DIGIT AND 3-DIGIT NUMBERS WITHOUT REGROUPING

Example 1: Add 123 + 64.

Solution: We place the digits in the hundreds, tens and ones columns.

	H	T	O
	1	2	3
+		6	4
	1	8	7

Ones Column: 3 + 4 = 7
Tens Column: 2 + 6 = 8
Hundreds Column: There is no digit under 1, so we write 1 in the hundreds place. So, 123 + 64 = 187.

So, 123 + 64 = **187**

In this case, we get a 3-digit number after adding a 2-digit number and a 3-digit number without carrying forward or regrouping.

Common Errors

	H	T	O
	1	2	0
+	4	9	

✗

	H	T	O
	1	2	0
+		4	9

✓

Go Easy!

It is easier to add 2-digit or 3-digit numbers by breaking them into hundreds, tens and ones. For example, 380 + 20 = 300 + 80 + 20 = (300 + 80) + 20 = 380 + 20 = 400

EXERCISE 5B

Add the following numbers.

1.

	H	T	O
	1	3	0
+		4	9

2.

	H	T	O
	1	2	3
+		3	1

3.

	H	T	O
	1	8	2
+		1	6

4.

	H	T	O
	2	0	4
+		7	3

ADDING 3-DIGIT NUMBERS WITHOUT REGROUPING

Let us see how we can add 3-digit numbers without carrying forward.

Adding Two 3-Digit Numbers

Example 1: Add 413 and 265.

Solution:

	H	T	O
	4	1	3
+	2	6	5
	6	7	8

Ones column,
3 + 5 = 8
Tens column:
1 + 6 = 7
Hundreds column:
4 + 2 = 6
So, 413 + 265 = 678

Adding Three 3-Digit Numbers

Example 2: Add 135, 212 and 321.

Solution:

	H	T	O
	1	3	5
	2	1	2
+	3	2	1
	6	6	8

Ones column:
5 + 2 + 1 = 8
Tens column:
3 + 1 + 2 = 6
Hundreds column:
1 + 2 + 3 = 6
So, 135 + 212 + 321 = 668.

EXERCISE 5C

Add the following.

1.

	H	T	O
	2	1	4
+	7	5	3

2.

	H	T	O
	5	2	6
+	3	7	3

3.

	H	T	O
	7	5	2
	1	0	0
+	1	2	1

4.

	H	T	O
	6	4	3
	2	1	2
+	1	1	3

LEARNING CORRECT PLACEMENT OF DIGITS

Placing the digits correctly is very important while adding numbers that have different number of digits.

Examples:

1. Solve 218 + 35.

	H	T	O
		1	
	2	1	8
+		3	5
	2	5	3

2. Solve 402 + 13 + 6.

	H	T	O
		1	
	4	0	2
		1	3
+			6
	4	2	1

Note

Write the numbers as per their place value and then add.

Place the digits as given below:

Ones digits of all numbers in the ones column

Tens digits of all numbers in the tens column

Hundreds digits of all numbers in the hundreds column

EXERCISE 5D

Place the digits correctly and add.

1. 222 + 50

H	T	O
+		

2. 317 + 41

H	T	O
+		

3. 441 + 105 + 10

H	T	O
+		

4. 112 + 13 + 2

H	T	O
+		

WORD PROBLEMS

Addition is done when:

1. a quantity increases by a given amount
2. we need to find the sum or total

Let us look at the following examples.

> **Note**
> Look out for addition words in problems. They can give a clue to solve the problem. Addition words: Add, total, altogether, sum, plus, more, increase, etc.

Example 1: Ram has two storybooks. One book has 235 pages. The other book has 123 pages. What is the total number of pages in both the books?

Solution:

	H	T	O	
One book has =	2	3	5	pages
The other book has =	+ 1	2	3	pages
	3	5	8	

So, the total number of pages in both the books are 358.

Example 2: There are 352 boys and 326 girls in a school. What is the total number of students in the school?

Solution:

	H	T	O
Boys =	3	5	2
Girls =	+ 3	2	6
	6	7	8

So, the total number of students are 678.

EXERCISE 5E

1. 243 people went to see a football match on Monday and 125 people went to see the match on Tuesday. How many people went to see the match on Monday and Tuesday?

	H	T	O
Monday =			
Tuesday = +			

_________ people went to see the match on Monday and Tuesday.

2. A bookshop has 240 English books and 154 Mathematics books. What is the total number of English and Mathematics books in the shop?

	H	T	O
English books =			
Mathematics books = +			

There are _________ English and Mathematics books in the shop.

3. An ice cream vendor sold 248 ice creams on Saturday and 231 ice creams on Sunday. How many ice creams did he sell on these two days?

	H	T	O
Saturday =			
Sunday = +			

The ice cream vendor sold _________ ice creams on these two days.

4. Ajoy has 134 red marbles, 264 green marbles and 300 blue marbles. What is the total number of marbles with Ajoy?

	H	T	O
Red marbles =			
Green marbles =			
Blue marbles = +			

The total number of marbles with Ajoy is _________.

Mental Maths

1. I am a 3-digit number. I have 2 in my ones place, 5 in my tens place and 8 in my hundreds place. If I add 1 to my ones place, 1 to my tens place and again a 1 to my hundreds place, what will I become? ____________________
2. 242 + 100 = __________
3. 163 + 101 = __________
4. 901 + 99 = __________

CROSSWORD

Fill in the digits in the squares below so that the sum of each side adds up to 500.

40	400	
		320
160	220	

Do you know?

We know that **plus** means to **add**.

'**Eleven plus two**' is 11 + 2 = **13** and

'**Twelve plus one**' = 12 + 1 = **13**

What do you observe?

The sum is 13 and there are 13 letters in both the phrases:

'**Eleven plus two**' and '**Twelve plus one**'.

Fun facts about the number 13!
Not so unlucky!!

1. In Greek mythology, Zeus was the thirteenth god and the most powerful one.
2. The number 13 is significantly represented at the Winchester Mystery House in San Jose: 13 bathrooms, 13 steps in the staircases, etc.
3. In certain countries, such as Belgium, some employees get a "13th month" pay cheque. So it is lucky for them!
4. In Italy, 13 is considered as a very lucky number. The expression, *fare tredici* ("to do 13") means hit the jackpot.

Maths Lab Activity

Aim: To learn addition of 2-digit and 3-digit numbers using flash cards.

Materials required: Flashcards numbered 1, 10, 20, 50 and 100

Procedure: 1. Make the following flash cards.

100 | 50 | 20 | 10 | 1

9 flash cards of 100 each [100]

10 flash cards of 50 each [50]

10 flash cards of 20 each [20]

10 flash cards of 10 each [10]

10 flash cards of 1 each [1]

2. Now make 2 teams.
3. Let one team give a 2-digit and a 3-digit numbers to the other team. The other team must calculate their sum and represent it in the form of flash cards.
4. The two teams can do this turn by turn.

Concept Map

Addition of bigger numbers

- Properties of addition
- Addition of bigger 2-digit numbers with regrouping
- Addition of 2-digit and 3-digit numbers without regrouping
- Addition of 3-digit numbers without regrouping
- Word problems
  - sum
  - in all
  - total
  - altogether

Key Concepts

- We learnt,
  - ➢ addition of bigger 2-digit numbers with regrouping,
  - ➢ addition of 2-and 3-digit numbers without regrouping,
  - ➢ addition of 3-digit numbers without regrouping
- **Word problems on addition:** Real-life situations where we need to understand the increase in bigger quantities or amounts.

Chapter Revision

A. Choose the correct option.

1. 54 + 29 = [79] [84] [83]
2. 145 + 22 = [167] [293] [193]

B. Fill in the blanks.

1. 300 + 400 = ________
2. 245 + 10 = 10 + ________ = ________
3. Adding 20 to 500 gives ________.
4. 78 + 55 = ________
5. 310, 410, 510, ______, ______, ______
6. 300 + 50 in words is ______________.

C. Add the following.

1.

	H	T	O
	5	3	4
+	2	1	2

2.

	H	T	O
	9	3	2
+		4	3

3.

	T	O
	2	0
	1	5
+	1	2

4.

	T	O
	2	5
	1	7
+	4	3

5.

	H	T	O
	1	0	3
	2	1	5
+	3	4	0

6.

	H	T	O
	3	0	0
	2	0	0
+	4	0	0

D. Match the following.

Column A	Column B
1. 100 + 400	One hundred seventy
2. 150 + 20	Two hundred sixty-five
3. 220 + 45	Four hundred eighty
4. 350 + 130	Five hundred

E. Write T for true and F for false.

1. Adding two 3-digit numbers can be a 2-digit number. [ ]
2. The sum of 600 and 25 is 652. [ ]
3. The sum of 201 and 30 is an even number. [ ]
4. Consider the numbers:

   200, 400, 600 and 800

   The sum of 100 and 700 is the fourth number given above. [ ]

F. Answer the following.

1. There are 250 tables and 122 chairs in a school. What is the total number of tables and chairs in the school?

	H	T	O
Tables =			
Chairs =	+		

The total number of tables and chairs is ____________.

2. In a rose garden, there were 368 plants of red roses and 331 plants of pink roses. What is the total number of rose plants in the garden?

	H	T	O
Red Roses =			
Pink Roses =	+		

The total number of rose plants is ____________.

3. A shopkeeper sold 12 dolls in one week and 39 dolls in the next week. Find the number of dolls he sold in both the weeks?

	H	T	O
Dolls sold in the first week =			
Dolls sold in the second week =	+		

The number of dolls that he sold in both the weeks was ____________.

4. 525 students participated in the Republic Day celebrations of a school. 43 more students volunteered to participate. How many students participated altogether?

	H	T	O
Number of students participated =			
Number of Volunteers =	+		

Altogether, __________ students participated.

SKILL UP!

Project

Visit a stationery shop and ask the prices of a notebook, an eraser and a pencil. Note down the prices and find out how much would you have to pay if you buy,

a. A pencil and an eraser
b. A notebook and an eraser
c. A notebook and a pencil
d. A notebook, a pencil and an eraser

Life Skills

In town A, there were 124 factories. In town, B there were 105 factories. These factories produced black smoke and polluted the air.

To clean the air, we need to stop the factories from producing black smoke. How many factories should be stopped? Do you think the air is getting polluted now-a-days to great extent? What do you think should be done to clean the air around us?

Mind Buzzer

1. Which of the following adds up to 987?

   a. 567 + 420
   b. 444 + 543
   c. 900 + 88
   d. 910 + 79

2. Find the missing digits.

	H	T	O
	2	4	__
	__	5	3
+	9	__	5
	__	__	__

Teacher's Notes

- The students can understand the properties of addition well.
- They can practise enough addition questions on addition of 3-digit numbers.
- Word problems on addition can help the students to understand the use of addition in daily life.

WORKSHEET

Solve the sums given in the balloons. Colour the balloons according to the given colour codes.

a. H T O
  2 1 4
+ 3 5 0

b. H T O
  1 2 3
+ 4 0 5

c. H T O
  1 0 4
+   2 5

d. H T O
  1 0 3
+ 2 1 5

e. H T O
  2 1 4
+ 1 5 0

f. H T O
  4 0 6
+ 3 1 2

g. H T O
  2 0 0
+ 3 0 1

h. H T O
  2 1 1
+   4 7

i. H T O
  5 7 2
+ 4 1 3

j. H T O
  2 4 7
+ 3 1 0

k. H T O
  9 1 4
+   2 3

Colour codes

Colour all balloons whose sum is between:

a. 700 and 999 - Red
b. 500 and 700 - Pink
c. 100 and 500 - Blue

6 Subtraction of Bigger Numbers

Learning Objectives

- To revise subtraction of 2-digit and 3-digit numbers from 3-digit numbers (without regrouping)
- To learn subtraction of 3-digit numbers (without regrouping)
- To learn how to place the digits of two numbers correctly while subtracting
- To practise word problems on subtraction

Let's Get Started

We learnt subtracting 2-digit numbers with borrowing in class 1. Let us recall.

1. There were 29 children playing in a park. Out of them, 15 were girls. How many boys were there?

Solution:

	T	O
Total number of children =	2	9
Number of girls =	− 1	5
Number of boys =	1	4

There were 14 boys.

2. Solve the following subtraction clouds.

16 less than 39 is?

T	O
3	9
− 1	6

39 − 16 = ______

Take away 52 from 68.

T	O
6	8
− 5	2

68 − 52 = ______

48 minus 26 is?

T	O
4	8
− 2	6

48 − 26 = ______

SUBTRACTION OF BIGGER NUMBERS WITHOUT REGROUPING

We have learnt about subtraction of 2-digit numbers from 3-digit numbers in chapter 3. Some students might find it difficult to build the concept, so let us revise.

Subtraction of 2-Digit Numbers from 3-Digit Numbers

For subtracting 2-digit numbers from 3-digit numbers, first subtract the ones digits, then the tens digits and finally retain the hundreds digit of the 3-digit number as it is.

Example: Out of 345 children in a class, 10 children were absent. How many children were present?

Solution:

	H	T	O
Total number of children =	3	4	5
Number of children absent =	–	1	0
			5

Step 1:

In the ones column, we subtract 0 from 5. We get 5 in the ones column.

	H	T	O
	3	4	5
–		1	0
		3	5

Step 2:

In the tens column, we subtract 1 from 4. We get 3 in the tens column.

	H	T	O
	3	4	5
–		1	0
	3	3	5

Step 3:

In the hundreds column, we have no digit to subtract from 3, hence we write, 3 in the hundreds column.

Therefore, 335 students were present.

More Examples:

1.

	H	T	O
	4	6	1
–		4	1
	4	2	0

2.

	H	T	O
	5	7	7
–		5	6
	5	2	1

Go Easy!

Write numbers according to their place values (one below the other) and then subtract.

PUZZLE!

Given that A = 222. Find the values of x, B and C as per the following.

a. x is a 2-digit number whose ones digit is equal to the tens digit.

b. C is a 3-digit number whose ones digit is 3.

c. A - x = C

d. A + x = B

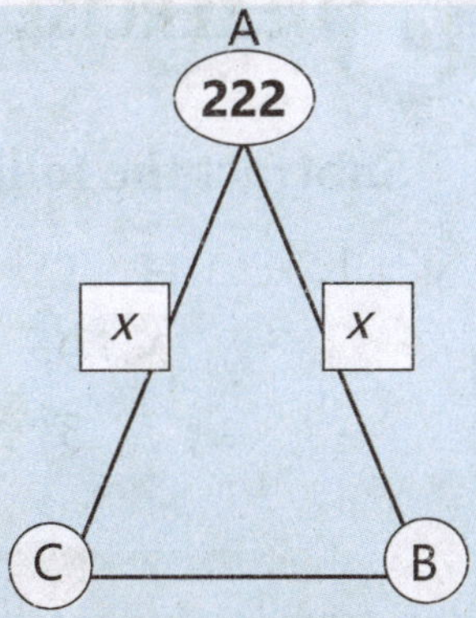

Subtraction of 3-Digit Numbers from 3-Digit Numbers

For subtracting 3-digit numbers from 3-digit numbers, first subtract the ones digits, then the tens digits and finally the hundreds digits.

Example: Radha bought some ice creams for ₹320. She gave ₹350 to the shopkeeper. How much money did she get in return from the shopkeeper?

Solution: We write this as a subtraction problem like,

Money given to the shopkeeper =
Cost of ice creams =

	H	T	O
	3	5	0
−	3	2	0
		3	0

The shopkeeper returned ₹30 to Radha.

Note

As we know, subtracting the same numbers gives the result as 0. If this happens in the hundreds column, we need not write 0 there.

More Examples:

1.

	H	T	O
	4	6	1
−	2	4	1
	2	2	0

2.

	H	T	O
	5	7	7
−	5	5	6
		2	1

3.

	H	T	O
	6	3	9
−	2	1	4
	4	2	5

4.

	H	T	O
	7	9	9
−	5	8	3
	2	1	6

Common Errors

The bigger number should always be on top while subtracting

	H	T	O
	1	3	8
−	3	4	2

✗

	H	T	O
	3	4	2
−	1	3	8

✓

EXERCISE 6A

Subtract the following.

1.

	H	T	O
	2	9	8
−		3	7

2.

	H	T	O
	3	4	5
−		2	0

3.

	H	T	O
	4	6	9
−	1	1	7

4.

	H	T	O
	8	7	4
−		6	3

LEARNING CORRECT PLACEMENT OF DIGITS

Just like addition, we must also learn to place the digits correctly before subtracting two numbers with different number of digits. Ones digits of both the numbers must be placed in the ones column (O), tens digits in the tens column (T) and hundreds digits in the hundreds column (H).

Example: Solve the following.

a. 355 – 35

	H	T	O
	3	5	5
–		3	5
	3	2	0

b. 467 – 5

	H	T	O
	4	6	7
–			5
	4	6	2

Common Errors

Solve 187 – 25.

✗

	H	T	O
	1	8	7
–	2	5	

✓

	H	T	O
	1	8	7
–		2	5

Digits must be placed according to their place values.

EXERCISE 6B

Place the digits correctly and subtract.

1. 522 – 11
2. 767 – 25
3. 589 - 61
4. 299 – 34

	H	T	O
–			

Mental Maths

1. Subtract 130 from 250. ____________
2. Subtract the smallest 3-digit number from 699. ____________
3. From 300, subtract the number that comes just after 199. ____________
4. _____ + 10 = 810
5. 654 – 1 = _______

Do you know?

There are different methods of subtraction followed in different countries. For example, Austrian Method, American Method, Subtraction from left to right which is unlike subtraction method that we follow from right to left, non-vertical methods, etc.

FIND THE MISSING DIGITS

When some digits are missing in our subtraction problems, we can find them using the rules given below.

a. To find the digit in first row, add the digits in the second and the third rows.
b. To find the digit in the second row, subtract the digit in the third row from the digit in the first row.

Example: Find the missing digits.

1.

	H	T	O
	5	7	8
−	3	6	3
	2	1	5

To find the missing digits,
Ones column: 8 − 5 = **3**
Tens column: 7 − 1 = **6**
Hundreds column:
5 − 2 = **3**

2.

	H	T	O
	7	8	9
−	4	2	4
	3	6	5

To find the missing digits,
Ones column: 9 − 5 = 4
Tens column: 2 + 6 = **8**
Hundreds column:
4 + 3 = **7**

EXERCISE 6C

Find the missing digits.

1.

	H	T	O
	8	9	4
−			
	2	7	3

2.

	H	T	O
	9	1	3
−			
	4	1	2

3.

	H	T	O
		7	
−	3		4
	2	7	2

4.

	H	T	O
			4
−	6	5	
	1	2	3

WORD PROBLEMS

Example 1: Niel planted 298 mango trees in his orchard. 124 trees died. How many trees were left in the orchard?

Solution:

Total number of trees =
Numbers of trees that died =

	H	T	O
	2	9	8
−	1	2	4
	1	7	4

174 trees were left.

Example 2: Siddharth's book had 375 pages. He read 142 pages. How many pages are left to be read?

Solution:

Total number of pages =
Pages read =

	H	T	O
	3	7	5
−	1	4	2
	2	3	3

233 pages are left to be read.

EXERCISE 6D

1. **A movie hall had 576 seats. 432 seats were occupied. How many seats were vacant?**

Total number of seats =
Number of seats occupied =

H	T	O
–		

_____________ seats were vacant.

2. **Anisha had 783 apples growing in her orchard. She plucked 532 apples out of them. How many apples were left?**

Total number of apples =
Apples plucked by Anisha =

H	T	O
–		

_____________ apples were left on the trees.

3. **John had 398 marbles. He lost 25 marbles. How many marbles were left with him?**

Total marbles =
Marbles lost =

H	T	O
–		

_____________ marbles were left with him.

4. **A bookshop had 963 books. 251 books got sold in one week. How many books were left in the shop?**

Total number of books =
Books sold =

H	T	O
–		

_____________ books were left in the shop.

Maths Lab Activity

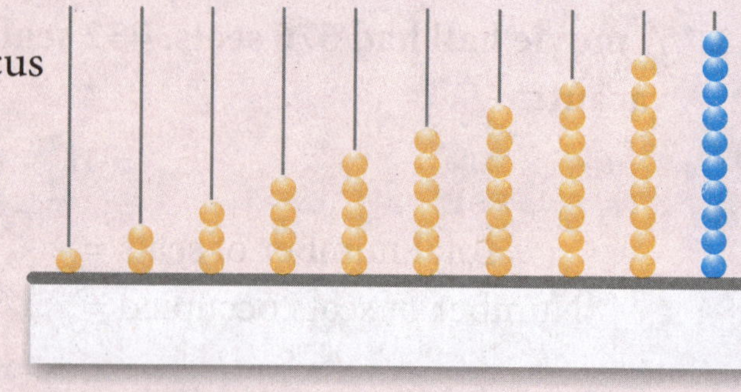

Aim: To solve subtraction problems using abacus

Materials required: Abacus

Procedure: Follow the steps below to solve subtraction problems using abacuses.

1. Let us solve 325 – 114.

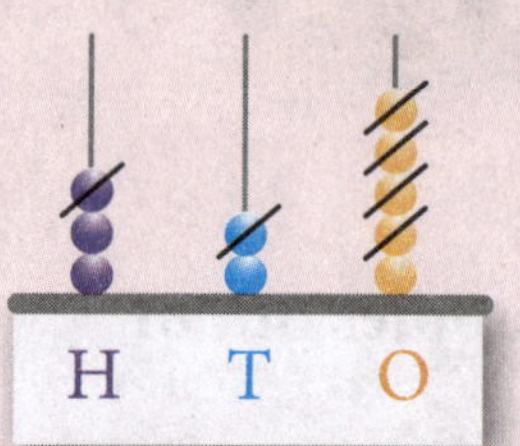

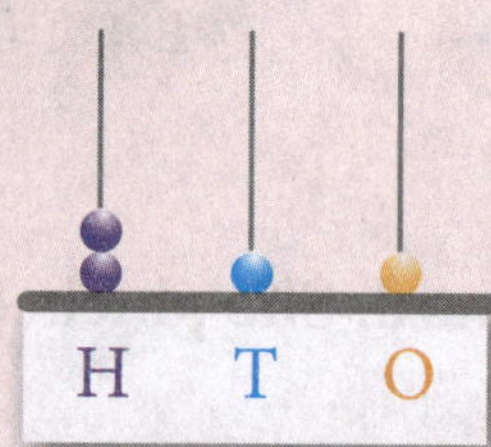

2. Take away 1 bead from the hundreds rod, 1 bead from the tens rod and 4 beads from the ones rod.

So, 325 - 114 = **211**

3. Now try the following subtraction problems on the abacus.

a. 356 – 120 b. 458 – 52 c. 343 – 111 d. 569 – 21

Concept Map

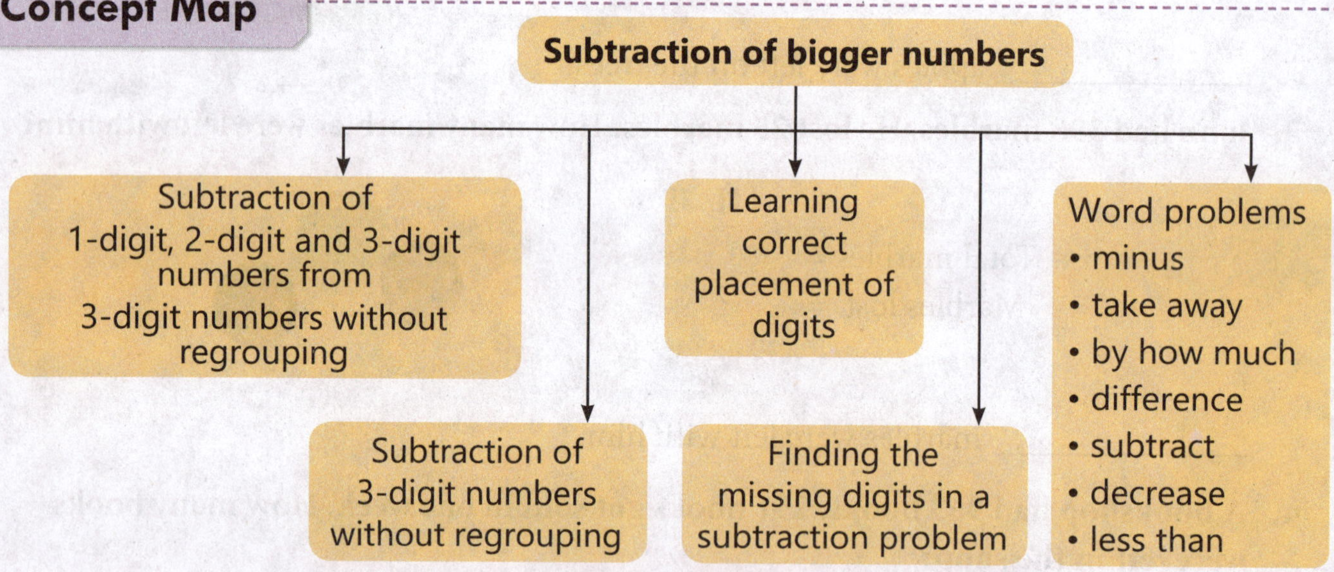

Key Concepts

- We revised the subtraction of 2-digit from 3-digit numbers without regrouping
- We learnt the subtraction of 3-digit numbers without regrouping
- **Word problems on subtraction:** This chapter involves word problems on subtraction with bigger numbers.

Chapter Revision

A. Choose the correct answer.

1. There were 334 sweets in a box. Bobby distributed 112 of them among his friends. How many sweets are left in the box?

   226   222   442   220

2. 456 taken away from 897 gives

   440   541   441   543

3. How much more is 999 than 865?

   143   140   130   134

B. Subtract the following.

1.

H	T	O
9	3	7
– 6	1	4

2.

H	T	O
8	6	3
– 5	2	0

3.

H	T	O
7	9	8
–	4	6

4.

H	T	O
6	8	9
– 4	2	9

C. Fill in the blanks.

1.

H	T	O
3	—	7
– —	5	—
2	0	7

2.

H	T	O
—	9	8
– 1	—	—
3	7	4

3.

H	T	O
8	7	—
– —	—	3
8	2	0

D. Place the digits correctly and solve.

1. 654 – 44

H	T	O
–		

2. 843 – 40

H	T	O
–		

3. 635 – 31

H	T	O
–		

E. Answer the following.

1. 455 children sat for an examination. 442 children passed the examination. How many children did not pass the examination?

   ____________ children did not pass the examination.

2. Samira had ₹895. She spent ₹753 out of it. How much money does Samira have now?

   Samira has ₹____________ now.

SKILL UP!

Project

Take a 2020 calendar. Count the number of days in every month. Add all of them. How many days are there in the whole year?

1. The total number of days is in between:

   a. 100 to 200   b. 200 to 300   c. 300 to 400   d. 400 to 500

2. How many less days than 999 are there in the whole year?

Life Skills

The government started free education for students whose parents could not pay. 342 students joined the free schools. When the schools started evening classes, the number of students increased to 978.

1. How many more students joined the schools after the evening classes started?
2. Should the government provide free schools for students whose parents can't pay?

Mind Buzzer

1. An ice cream vendor sold 200 ice creams on Monday and 201 ice creams the next day. How many more ice creams did he sell on Tuesday?
2. There are some juice bottles in a big box. Pinky added four more juice bottles. Now there are 267 juice bottles. How many juice bottles were there in the beginning?

Teacher's Notes

- The students can understand the properties of subtraction by practising subtraction problems.
- Practising questions can help the students to place the digits of the numbers being subtracted in the correct manner. This will also help them to understand that bigger numbers are placed above while solving vertical subtraction problems.

WORKSHEET

Look at the heights of these sunflowers and answer the questions that follow.

1. How much taller is Sunflower A than Sunflower B? ____________ units
2. How much taller is sunflower B than Sunflower C? ____________ units
3. If sunflower D grows to be the same height as Sunflower A, how many more units will it need to grow? ____________ units
4. What is the difference in height between Sunflower D and Sunflower E? ____________ units
5. How much shorter is Sunflower E than Sunflower B? ____________ units.

REASONING WORKSHEET 1

1. **A car parking area outside a shopping complex can accommodate 80 cars. Which of the following is true for car accommodation?**

   a. 140 cars b. 81 cars c. 71 cars d. 59 cars

2. **Anu collected (294 + 105) fruit stickers. Bill collected (300 + 99) fruit stickers. Which is true?**

   a. Anu has more stickers

   b. The sum of stickers with Anu and Bill is 798

   c. Bill has more stickers

   d. Anu and Bill have equal number of stickers

3. **Write the 3-digit number using the following clues.**

   - **The ones digit is 7.**
   - **When 155 is subtracted from the number, the result is 42.**

   a. 197 b. 179 c. 113 d. 117

4. **A train has (130 + 157) seats. How many people can sit in the train?**

   a. 400 b. 300 c. 280 d. 387

5. **I have ₹ (785 – 510) . What can be the price/prices of the dress that I can afford to buy?**

   $$\begin{array}{r} 7\ 8\ 5 \\ -\ 5\ 1\ 0 \\ \hline \end{array}$$

   a. ₹250 b. ₹300 c. ₹375 d. ₹200

6. **Given that each  = 100,**

   each  = 10 and

   each  = 1

   Given below is the appropriate representation of which 3-digit number?

   a. 285 b. 295 c. 293 d. 290

7 Multiplication

Learning Objectives

- To learn multiplication tables of 1, 2, 3, 4, 5 and 10
- To solve repeated addition in a shorter time by using multiplication
- To learn the terms used in multiplication and multiplication on number line
- To learn horizontal and vertical methods of multiplication
- To learn multiplication of 2- and 3-digit numbers with 1-digit numbers without regrouping
- To learn multiplication of 2-digit numbers with 1-digit numbers with regrouping
- To solve word problems

Let's Get Started

The maths teacher of a class gave a few multiplication problems to three students. Each student was supposed to find the product of two problems.

1. How many problems were solved by the students?
2. Can we use repeated addition to solve them?

Let us find out.

Number of students = 3

Number of problems to be solved = 2

This can be written as:

Total number of problems = 2 + 2 + 2 = 3 × 2 = **6**

Hence, the students solved a total of 6 multiplication problems.

WHAT IS MULTIPLICATION?

Whenever a quantity increases, we either add or multiply. When a number increases by a certain amount, we add but **when a number increases many times of itself, we multiply**.

Example: $3 \times 4 = \mathbf{12}$. We can say that 3 **times** 4 is 12.

12 is also called the **product** in the multiplication statement.

> $\times$ is the symbol of multiplication.

> **Note**
> To find the product means to multiply.
> The word 'times' refers to multiplication.

MULTIPLICATION AS REPEATED ADDITION

As we learned earlier, multiplication is also referred to as repeated addition. When we need to add the same number to itself a number of times, we can calculate it faster using multiplication.

Consider 3 groups of stars.

Number of groups = 3

Number of stars in each group = 6

Therefore, $3 \times 6 = \mathbf{18}$.

EXERCISE 7A

1. Fill in the blanks and write the multiplication statements.

a.  = ______ × ______ = ______

b. 

= ______________ × ______________ = ______________

2. Write the multiplication statements for the following repeated additions.

a. 3 + 3 + 3 + 3 + 3 + 3 + 3 = ______ × ______ = ______

b. 7 + 7 + 7 + 7 = ______ × ______ = ______

c. 4 + 4 + 4 + 4 + 4 + 4 = ______ × ______ = ______

d. 9 + 9 + 9 = ______ × ______ = ______

3. **Match the pictures in column A with the multiplication facts in column B.**

Column A	Column B
a. 	$4 \times 8 =$ _____
b. 	$9 \times 3 =$ _____
c. 	$4 \times 5 =$ _____
d. 	$3 \times 6 =$ _____

TERMS USED IN MULTIPLICATION

A multiplication statement consists of three numbers.

Two numbers are multiplied to give a **product**.

The two numbers being multiplied are called the **multiplier** and the **multiplicand**.

Example: 3 × 2 = 6

- 3 → Multiplier (or Multiplicand)
- 2 → Multiplicand (or Multiplier)
- 6 → Product

Note

1. In a multiplication statement, the order of the numbers being multiplied does not change the answer.

   2 × 1 = 2, 1 × 2 = 2

2. If a number is multiplied with 1, the value of the number does not change; it remains the same.

   2 × 1 = 2, 8 × 1 = 8

3. If a number is multiplied with 0, the value of the number becomes 0.

   3 × 0 = 0, 7 × 0 = 0

MULTIPLICATION TABLES

Table of 1

Let us make the table of 1 by counting the number of toffees in each row.

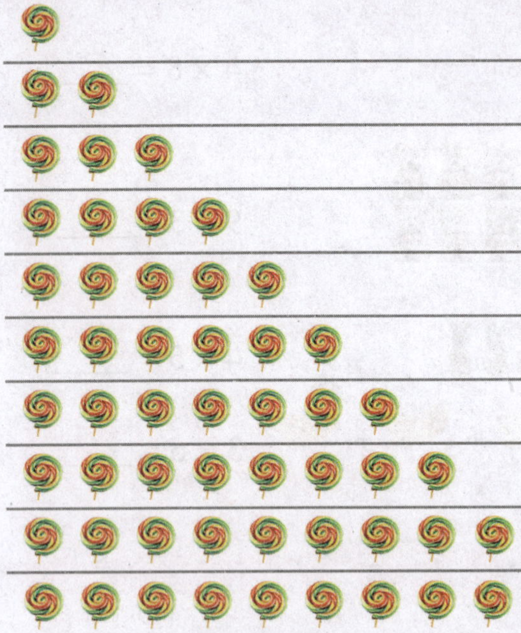

$1 \times 1 = 1$

$2 \times 1 = 2$

$3 \times 1 = 3$

$4 \times 1 = 4$

$5 \times 1 = 5$

$6 \times 1 = 6$

$7 \times 1 = 7$

$8 \times 1 = 8$

$9 \times 1 = 9$

$10 \times 1 = 10$

When we add 1 to a number, it increases by 1. So, we can form a table of 1 where the product increases by 1 every time.

Note

1 × 5 = **5** is read as
1 multiplied by 5 is equal to 5.

Table of 2

Let us make the table of 2 by counting twin babies in each row.

$1 \times 2 = 2$

$2 \times 2 = 4$

$3 \times 2 = 6$

$4 \times 2 = 8$

$5 \times 2 = 10$

$6 \times 2 = 12$

$7 \times 2 = 14$

$8 \times 2 = 16$

$9 \times 2 = 18$

$10 \times 2 = 20$

When we add 2 to a number, it increases by 2. So, we can form a table of 2 where the product increases by 2 every time.

Note

The products in the table of 2 end with 0, 2, 4, 6 or 8.

Table of 3

Count the number of wheels in each tricycle in each row to make the table of 3.

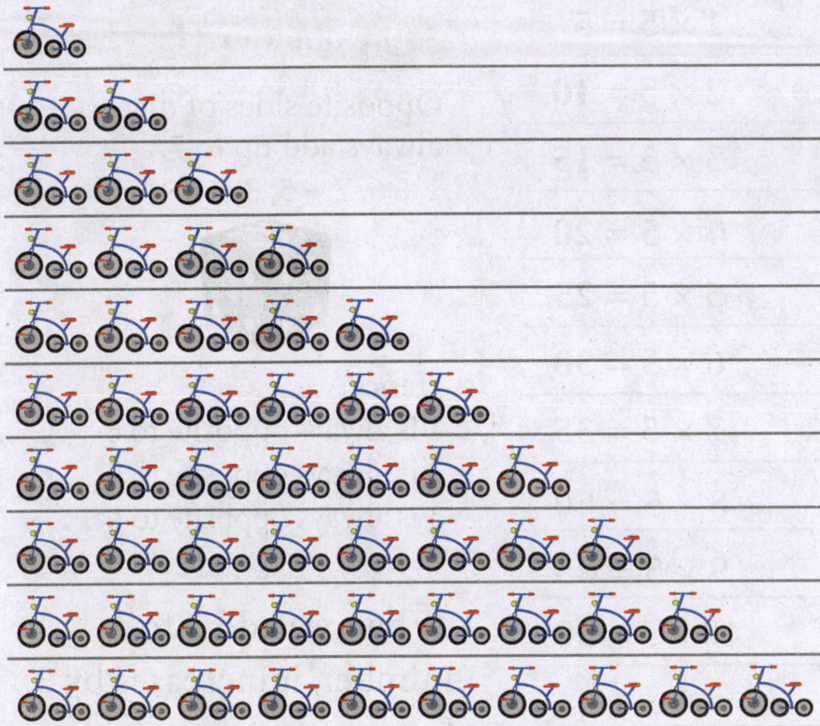

1 tricycle	$1 \times 3 = \mathbf{3}$
2 tricycles	$2 \times 3 = \mathbf{6}$
3 tricycles	$3 \times 3 = \mathbf{9}$
4 tricycles	$4 \times 3 = \mathbf{12}$
5 tricycles	$5 \times 3 = \mathbf{15}$
6 tricycles	$6 \times 3 = \mathbf{18}$
7 tricycles	$7 \times 3 = \mathbf{21}$
8 tricycles	$8 \times 3 = \mathbf{24}$
9 tricycles	$9 \times 3 = \mathbf{27}$
10 tricycles	$10 \times 3 = \mathbf{30}$

When we add 3 to a number, it increases by 3. So, we can form a table of 3 where the product increases by 3 every time.

Table of 4

Count the mathematical symbols in each row and make the table of 4.

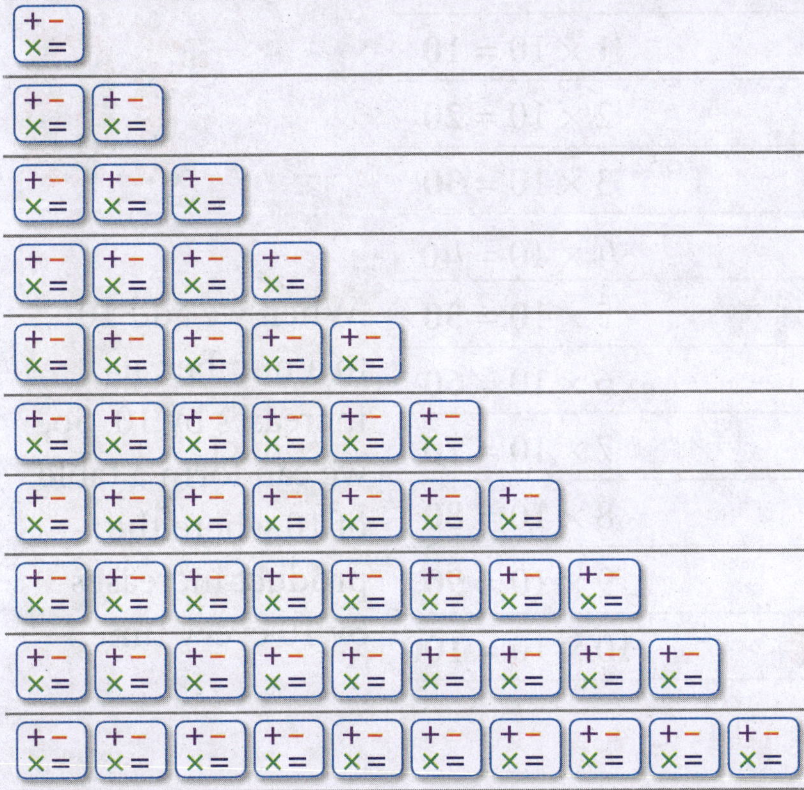

1 tile	$1 \times 4 = \mathbf{4}$
2 tiles	$2 \times 4 = \mathbf{8}$
3 tiles	$3 \times 4 = \mathbf{12}$
4 tiles	$4 \times 4 = \mathbf{16}$
5 tiles	$5 \times 4 = \mathbf{20}$
6 tiles	$6 \times 4 = \mathbf{24}$
7 tiles	$7 \times 4 = \mathbf{28}$
8 tiles	$8 \times 4 = \mathbf{32}$
9 tiles	$9 \times 4 = \mathbf{36}$
10 tiles	$10 \times 4 = \mathbf{40}$

When we add 4 to a number, it increases by 4. So, we can form a table of 4 where the product increases by 4 every time.

Table of 5

Count the number of dots on each dice in each row and make the table of 5.

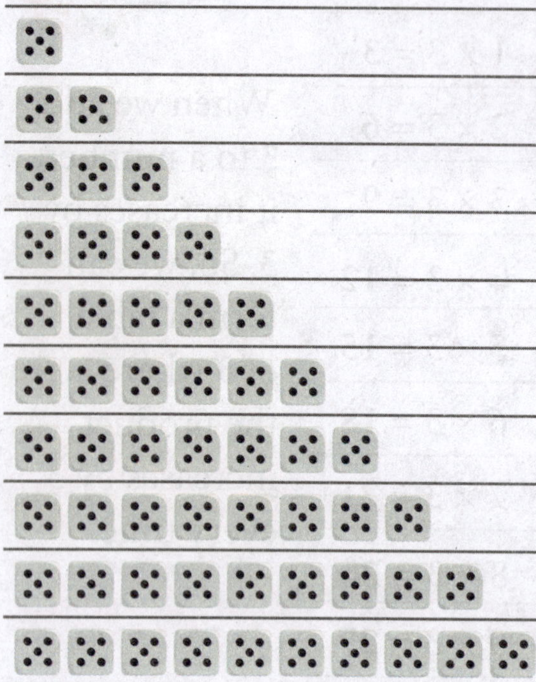

	1 × 5 = **5**
	2 × 5 = **10**
	3 × 5 = **15**
	4 × 5 = **20**
	5 × 5 = **25**
	6 × 5 = **30**
	7 × 5 = **35**
	8 × 5 = **40**
	9 × 5 = **45**
	10 × 5 = **50**

Do you know?

Opposite sides of dice always add up to 7.
1 + 6, 2 + 5, 3 + 4

Hence,
1 is always opposite to 6
2 is always opposite to 5
3 is always opposite to 4

When we add 5 to a number, it increases by 5. So, we can form a table of 5 where the product increases by 5 every time.

Table of 10

Count the number of colours shown in each row and make the table of 10.

	1 × 10 = **10**
	2 × 10 = **20**
	3 × 10 = **30**
	4 × 10 = **40**
	5 × 10 = **50**
	6 × 10 = **60**
	7 × 10 = **70**
	8 × 10 = **80**
	9 × 10 = **90**
	10 × 10 = **100**

When we add 10 to a number, it increases by 10. So, we can form a table of 10 where the product increases by 10 every time.

EXERCISE 7B

1. Learn the multiplication tables of 1, 2, 3, 4, 5 and 10 and write them in your notebook.

2. Complete the following.

a. $3 \times 2 =$ ______ $\times 3$ b. $5 \times 2 =$ ______ $\times 5$ c. $2 \times 1 =$ ______

d. $4 \times 4 =$ ______ e. $6 \times 10 =$ ______ f. $5 \times 5 =$ ______

g. $7 \times 5 =$ ______ h. $0 \times 2 =$ ______ i. $9 \times 4 =$ ______

j. $1 \times 0 =$ ______ k. $8 \times 3 =$ ______ l. $8 \times 4 =$ ______

m. $2 \times 10 = 10 \times 2 =$ ______ n. $4 \times 5 = 5 \times 4 =$ ______ o. $3 \times 4 = 4 \times 3 =$ ______

3. Fill in the blanks.

a. In $2 \times 5 = 10$,

The multiplier is ________

The multiplicand is ________

The product is ________

b. In $7 \times 5 = 35$,

The multiplier is ________

The multiplicand is ________

The product is ________

PUZZLE!

Pick up a dice.

1. Find out how many dots are there opposite to five dots ____________.
2. Multiply the answer of the above question by 3. What do we get? ____________

NUMBER LINE

A number line represents numbers in order. As we move to the right, the numbers increase and as we move to the left, the numbers decrease. Let us learn the multiplication tables using number line.

Table of 1 on a number line is shown as below:

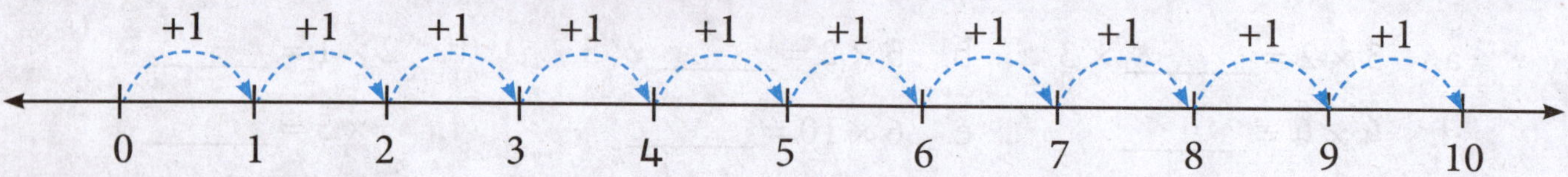

In the table of 1, the numbers increase by 1 every time. Look at the jumps of 1.

Table of 2 on a number line is shown as below:

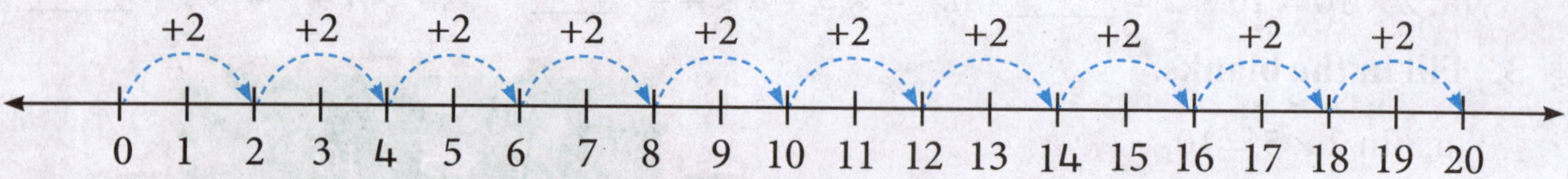

In the table of 2, the numbers increase by 2 every time. Look at the jumps of 2.

Table of 3 on a number line is shown as below:

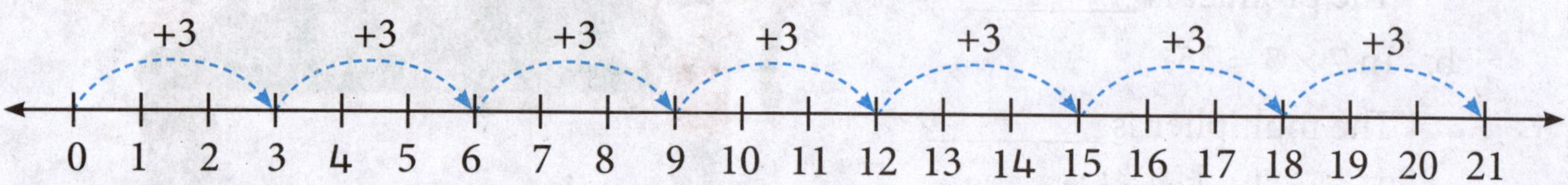

In the table of 3, the numbers increase by 3 every time. Look at the jumps of 3.

Table of 4 on a number line is shown as below:

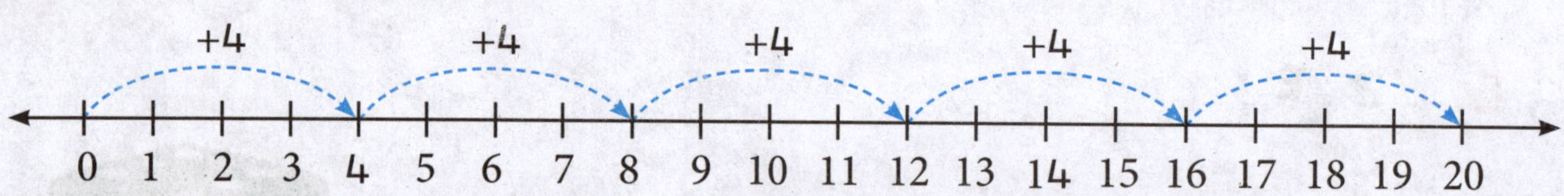

In the table of 4, the numbers increase by 4 every time. Look at the jumps of 4.

Table of 5 on a number line is shown as below:

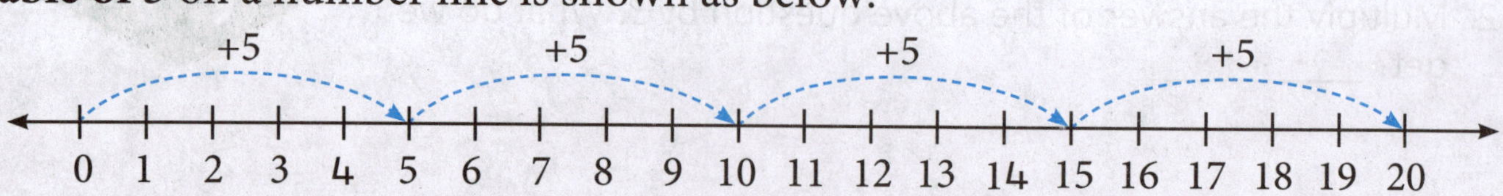

In the table of 5, the numbers increase by 5 every time. Look at the jumps of 5.

Table of 10 on a number line is shown as below:

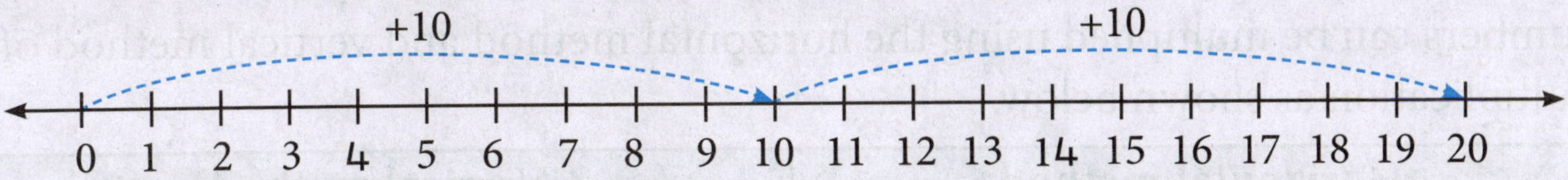

In the table of 10, the numbers increase by 10 every time. Look at the jumps of 10.

DOUBLES

Two times any number **doubles** the number.

Bobby ate 3 doughnuts. She wants to double the number of doughnuts to eat.

This means, she wants to eat 3 more doughnuts, that is, $3 + 3 = 6$ doughnuts.

How can we find the double of a number? We can find the double of a number by

- multiplying it by 2 or
- adding the number to itself

Examples:

1. Write the double of 3.

   a. $3 \times 2 = \mathbf{6}$ or

   b. $3 + 3 = \mathbf{6}$

This means double of 3 is 6.

2. Write the double of 10.

   a. $10 \times 2 = \mathbf{20}$ or

   b. $10 + 10 = \mathbf{20}$

This means double of 10 is 20.

EXERCISE 7C

1. Multiply the given numbers using number line and write the answer.

a. $2 \times 5 =$ ______

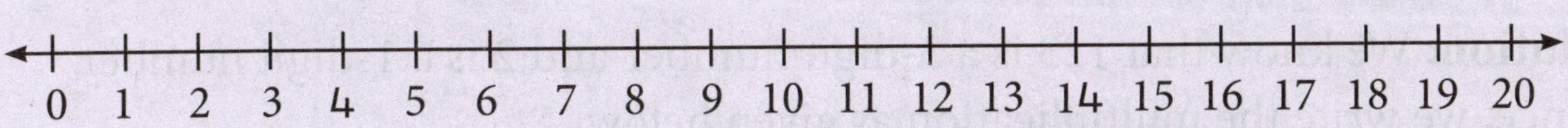

b. $4 \times 3 =$ ______

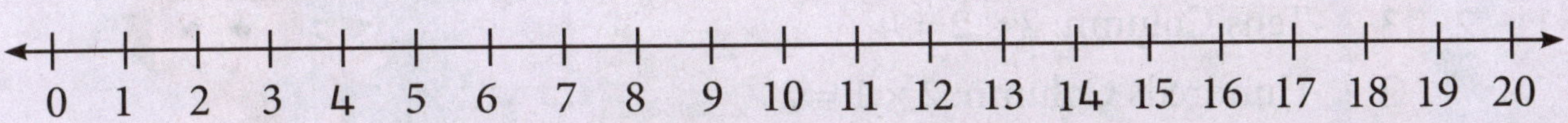

2. Find the double of:

a. 7 b. 5 c. 26 d. 330

HORIZONTAL AND VERTICAL METHOD OF MULTIPLICATION

Numbers can be multiplied using the horizontal method and vertical method of multiplication as shown below.

Horizontal method	Vertical method
4 × 5 = **20**, 7 × 10 = **70**	(see below)

Vertical method:

	T	O
		4
×		5
	2	**0**

	T	O
	1	0
×		7
	7	**0**

MULTIPLICATION OF 2-DIGIT AND 3-DIGIT NUMBERS WITH 1-DIGIT NUMBERS WITHOUT REGROUPING

Example 1: Multiply 13 × 2.

Solution: We know that, 13 is a 2-digit number and 2 is a 1-digit number.

Hence, we write the multiplication as given below.

> **Note**
> We must remember the multiplication tables very well for finding the product of two numbers.

	T	O
	1	3
×		2
		6

Step 1: First multiply 2 with 3 in the ones column,

that is, 2 × 3 = **6**.

Write 6 under 2 in the ones column.

	T	O
	1	3
×		2
	2	6

Step 2: Multiply 2 with 1 in the tens column,

that is, 2 × 1 = **2**. Write 2 in the tens column before 6.

So, 13 × 2 = **26**.

Example 2: Multiply 123 × 2.

Solution: We know that 123 is a 3-digit number and 2 is a 1-digit number. Hence, we write the multiplication as given below.

	H	T	O
	1	2	3
×			2
	2	4	6

Ones Column: 2 × 3 = **6**

Tens Column: 2 × 2 = **4**

Hundreds Column: 2 × 1 = **2**

So, 123 × 2 = **246**.

Mental Maths

1. 200 × 2 = ☐ 2. 50 × 2 = ☐ 3. 40 × 8 = ☐ 4. 30 × 3 = ☐

Go Easy!

When we multiply a number with a number ending with 0, we can use a shorter method explained below.

Example: Multiply 30 × 2

30 has one 0, we write 0 at the end of the answer. 30 × 2 = __0

Now multiply the other digits, 3 and 2, 3 × 2 = 6. So, we write 6 before 0.

That is, 30 × 2 = 60

In the same way, 300 × 2 = 600, 400 × 2 = 800, 200 × 5 = 1000, etc.

EXERCISE 7D

Find the products.

1.

	T	O
		9
×		5

2.

	T	O
	1	0
×		5

3.

	T	O
	5	6
×		1

4.

H	T	O
4	3	0
×		2

MULTIPLICATION OF 2-DIGIT NUMBERS WITH 1-DIGIT NUMBERS WITH REGROUPING

Example: Multiply 26 × 3.

Solution: We can write the multiplication as given below.

	T	O
	2	6
×		3

Step 1: First multiply 3 with 6 in the ones column.

3 × 6 = **18**

	T	O
	1	
	2	6
×		3
		8

Step 2: Write 8 of 18 in the ones column under 3 and carry forward 1 of 18. Write this 1 above 2 in the tens column.

	T	O
	1	
	2	6
×		3
	7	8

Step 3: Now, multiply 3 with 2 in the tens column.

3 × 2 = **6**. Add the carried forward 1 to 6.

6 + 1 = **7**. Write 7 in the tens column, before 8.

So, 26 × 3 = **78**.

Common Errors

	T	O
	1	
	1	7
×		2
	2	4

✗

	T	O
	1	
	1	7
×		2
	3	4

✓

EXERCISE 7E

Multiply the following.

1.

	T	O
	1	6
×		2

2.

	T	O
	2	8
×		3

3.

	T	O
	1	2
×		8

4.

	T	O
	3	7
×		2

5.

	T	O
	4	5
×		4

WORD PROBLEMS

In word problems, whenever the answer increases, we **add** or **multiply**.

- When the answer increases exactly by the number given in the question, we **add**.
- When the answer increases many times by the number given in the question, we **multiply**.
- When the value of one item is given and we need to find the value of more items, we **multiply**.

Let us solve the following examples.

Example 1: One tricycle has 3 wheels. How many wheels are there in 5 tricycles?

Solution: Number of wheels in 1 tricycle = 3

Number of wheels in 5 tricycles = 5 × 3 = **15**

There are 15 wheels in 5 tricycles.

Example 2: A baker sells 134 cakes in one day. How many cakes does she sell in 2 days?

Solution: Number of cakes sold in 1 day = 134

Number of cakes sold in 2 days = 134 × 2

She sells 268 cakes in 2 days.

	H	T	O
	1	3	4
×			2
	2	6	8

EXERCISE 7F

1. **In a classroom, 6 children sit in one row. How many children can sit in 3 rows?**

Number of children in 1 row = ☐

Number of children in 3 rows = ☐ × ☐

= ☐

☐ children can sit in 3 rows.

2. **One box has 9 pieces of cookies in it. How many pieces of cookies are there in 5 boxes?**

Number of pieces in 1 box = ☐

Number of pieces in 5 boxes = ☐ × ☐

= ☐

☐ pieces of cookies are there in 5 boxes.

3. **A shopkeeper sells 323 shirts in one month. How many shirts does he sell in two months?**

Number of shirts sold in 1 month = ☐

Number of shirts sold in 2 months = ☐ × ☐

= ☐

He sells ☐ shirts in 2 months.

4. **230 people can sit in one train. How many people can sit in 3 trains?**

Number of people in 1 train = ☐

Number of people in 3 trains = ☐ × ☐

= ☐

☐ people can sit in 3 trains.

5. A box of erasers costs ₹45. How much do 6 boxes of erasers cost?

Cost of 1 eraser box = ₹ ☐

Cost of 6 eraser boxes = ☐ × ☐

= ₹ ☐

6 boxes of erasers will cost ₹ ☐.

Mental Maths

1. 3 + 3 + 3 + 3 = _____ × 3 = _____.
2.  = 2 × 5 = _____.
3. Multiplier × Multiplicand = ________________
4. a. 4 × 0 = _____ b. 7 × 0 = _____
5. a. 6 × 1 = _____ b. 9 × 1 = _____
6. a. 3 × 5 = _____ b. 2 × 600 = _____
7. 1 × 2 = 2 × _____
8. Four multiplied by two is = 4 × _____ = _____
9. Double of 5 gives _____.
10. 10 × 2 gives double of _____.

Maths Lab Activity

Aim: Construction of multiplication tables of 2, 3, 4 and 5 using ice cream sticks.

Materials required: Ice cream sticks

Procedure: To multiply 3 with 3,

1. Put 3 sticks horizontally for the first number.

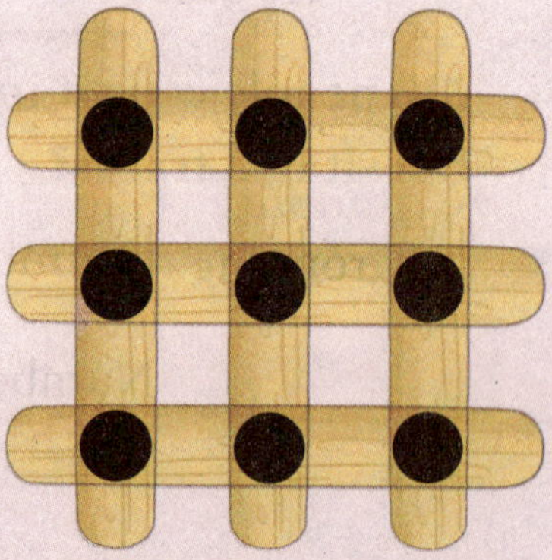

2. Now put 3 sticks vertically for the second number.
3. Now count the number of points where the sticks meet (encircled in black).

The number of points is 9, so the answer is 3 × 3 = **9**.

Concept Map

- **Multiplication**
  - Multiplication as repeated addition
  - Properties of multiplication
  - Multiplication tables of 1, 2, 3, 4, 5 and 10
  - Multiplication using number line
  - Multiplication of 2-digit and 3-digit numbers with 1-digit numbers without regrouping
  - Multiplication of 2-digit and 1-digit numbers with regrouping
  - Word problems
    - increase many times
    - find the value of more items

Key Concepts

- **Multiplication:** When a number increases many times of itself, we multiply.
- **Repeated addition:** Adding the same number many times
- **Multiplicand:** The number to be multiplied
- **Multiplier:** The number which determines the number of times the multiplicand is to be multiplied
- **Product:** The result of multiplication of two numbers
- Multiplication with 0 gives 0 always. Multiplication with 1 gives the number itself.
- To **double** a number, multiply the number by 2 or add the number to itself.
- Numbers can be multiplied horizontally as well as vertically.
- We learnt,
  - ➢ Multiplication of 2- and 3-digit numbers with 1-digit numbers without regrouping
  - ➢ Multiplication of 2-digit numbers with 1-digit numbers with regrouping
- **Word problems on multiplication:** Getting familiar with real-life applications of multiplication

Chapter Revision

A. Complete the table.

Multiplication Statement	Multiplier	Multiplicand	Product
1. 6 × 7	______	______	______
2. 0 × 10	______	______	______
3. 1 × 9	______	______	______
4. 5 × 5	______	______	______

B. Choose the correct option.

1. 2 × 5
   a. 11 b. 12 c. 10 d. 25
2. 10 × 4
   a. 40 b. 14 c. 10 d. 4
3. 7 × 7
   a. 17 b. 49 c. 70 d. 7
4. 4 × 90
   a. 36 b. 63 c. 630 d. 360

C. Fill the missing terms using multiplication tables.

1. 4, _____, _____, 16, _____
2. 7, _____, 21, _____, 35
3. 3, _____, _____, 12, 15
4. 9, 18, _____, _____, _____

D. Fill in the blanks.

1. 4 times 6 is _______
2. The products in the table of 2 end with _______, _______, _______, _______ or 8.
3. The products in the table of 5 end with _______ and _______ alternatively.
4. The products in the table of 10 end with _______.

E. Find the product.

1. 30 × 2 = _____
2. 40 × 5 = _____
3. 4 × 2 = _____
4. 5 × 3 = _____
5. 8 × 5 = _____
6. 9 × 1 = _____
7. 4 × 0 = _____
8. 6 × 10 = _____

F. Answer the following.

1. Dhruv eats 4 sandwiches every day. How many sandwiches can he eat in 8 days?
2. A lunch box costs ₹120. How much will be the cost of 3 lunch boxes?
3. If 5 people can sit in one car, how many people can sit in 16 cars?

SKILL UP!

Project

1. Count the number of students in your class. Write a multiplication statement for the total number of students. Can you write more than one multiplication statements?
2. Count the number of family members in your best friend's family. Add that number to the number of family members in your family. Now, write the multiplication statements for the total number of family members.

Life Skills

Madhu's mother wanted to give stationery to the school children whose parents could not afford to buy it. The school teacher told her that they needed the following items.

Help Madhu's mother to find out the exact amount of money needed.

Do you think Madhu's mother is kind-hearted? Have you helped anyone in any way? Specify.

Stationery items	Quantity	Cost of 1 item (₹)	Total cost
Notebook	9	20	9 × 20
Pencil	8	3	8 × 3
Eraser	7	4	7 × 4
Sharpener	6	5	6 × 5
Pencil box	5	10	5 × 10

Mind Buzzer

1. I am a 3-digit number. I am the result of 2 multiplied by a number which is 1 more than 243. What number am I?
2. Rajat is 5 years old. Meena is 2 × 3 years older than Rajat. How old is Meena?

Teacher's Notes

- Multiplication is a concept that students can understand easily when explained as repeated addition. When the students are made to see it practically by making groups among themselves, they enjoy it.
- Learning the multiplication tables thoroughly can help the children solve multiplication problems easily.
- They can understand multiplication with zero and multiplication with 1 by practising exercise questions.
- While regrouping, if the students write the carried forward number in a circle (to highlight) on top, it will help them in not making mistakes.

WORKSHEET

Radha joined a new school.

She needed to buy the following items. The different costs of items are multiplied by their respective quantities to get the final prices. Fill in the blanks.

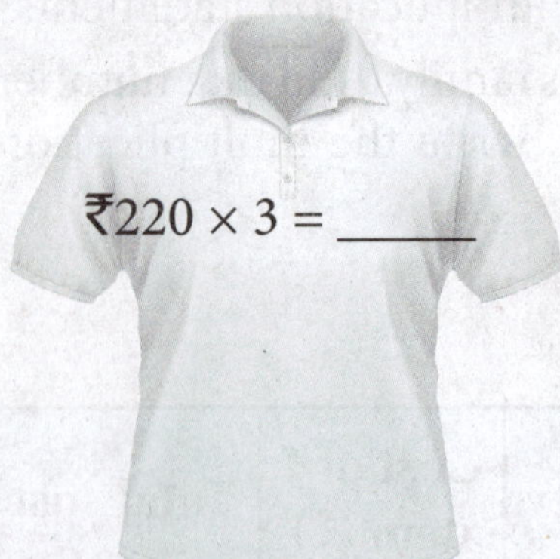

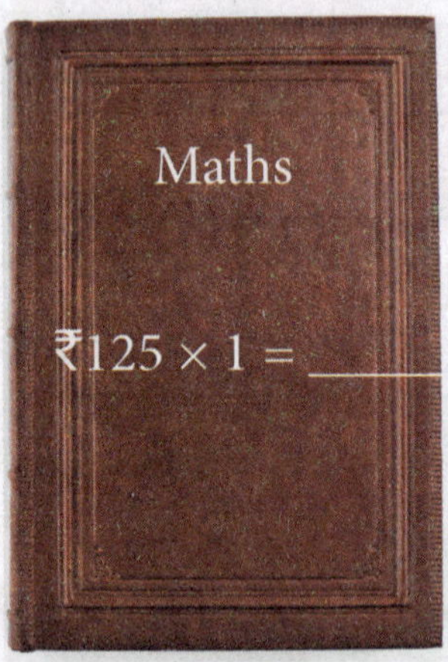

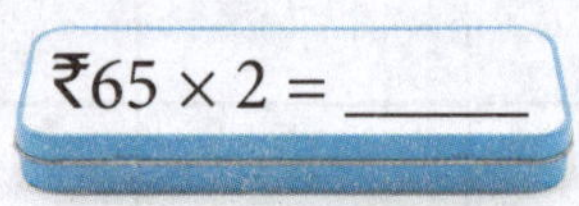

Find the products given on each item.

How much money did she spend on each item?

1. Shirts = ₹ ________
2. Skirts = ₹ ________
3. Books = ₹ ________
4. Pencil boxes = ₹ ________
5. Lunch boxes = ₹ ________

8 Division

Learning Objectives

- To understand division as equal sharing, equal grouping and repeated subtraction
- To understand division on the number line
- To understand the terms used in division and properties of division

Let's Get Started

Ankit has 6 balloons. He wants to distribute these balloons equally among him and his two friends.

Look at the picture below. Has Amit distributed the balloons equally among him and his friends?

____

Each child should get ________ balloons.

DIVISION AS EQUAL SHARING

Division can be explained as equal sharing. Share 8 toffees among 4 children such that each child gets the same number of toffees.

We find that when we share 8 toffees equally among 4 boys, then each boy gets 2 toffees and there are no toffees left.

This can be explained by the following division statement.

> **Note**
>
> ÷ is the symbol of division.

8	÷	4	=	2
Total number of toffees		Number of boys		Number of toffees with each boy

Example: Share 9 bananas equally among 3 monkeys.

9 bananas

9 ÷ 3 = 3. One monkey gets 3 bananas.

DIVISION AS EQUAL GROUPING

Division can also be explained as equal grouping.

Put 10 pencils in equal groups of 2 each.

We find that when we make groups of 2 each out of 10 pencils, we get 5 groups.

This can be explained by the following division statement.

10 ÷ 2 = 5

Example: Put 12 stars in equal groups of 6 each.

How many groups do you get? 12 ÷ 6 = ☐

EXERCISE 8A

1. **Share 12 apples equally among 4 children.**

Each child will get ______ apples.

$12 \div 4 = \square$

2. **Share 6 bones equally between 2 dogs.**

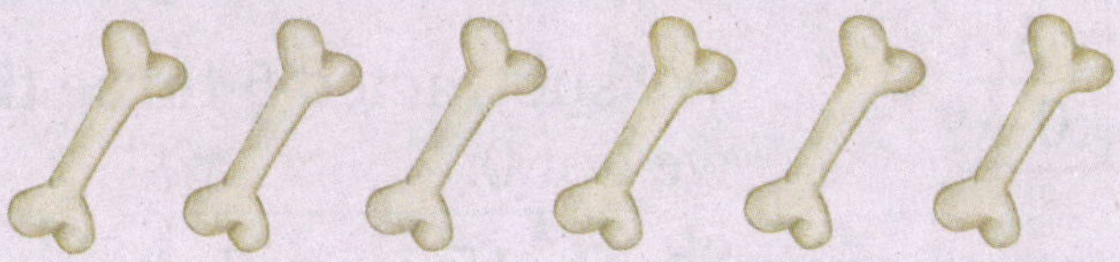

Each dog will get ______ bones.

$6 \div 2 = \square$

3. **Share 12 pieces of cheese equally among 3 mice.**

Each mouse will get ______ pieces of cheese.

$12 \div 3 = \square$

4. **Put 14 balls in equal groups of 7.**

How many balls are there in one group?

$14 \div 7 = \square$

5. **Put 15 butterflies in equal groups of 5.**

How many butterflies are there in one group?

$15 \div 5 = \square$

DIVISION AS REPEATED SUBTRACTION

Division can also be explained as repeated subtraction.

Example 1: 12 ÷ 3 = ☐

To get the answer to this, we subtract 3 from 12 and keep subtracting 3 from the answer till we get 0.

Then, we count the number of times 3 is subtracted. That will be our answer.

12
−3 → 9 (1)
−3 → 6 (2)
−3 → 3 (3)
−3 → 0 (4)

We subtracted 3 **four times** till we got 0.

So, $12 \div 3 = 4$

Example 2: 15 ÷ 5 = ☐

15
−5 → 10 (1)
−5 → 5 (2)
−5 → 0 (3)

We subtracted 5 **three times** till we got 0.

So, $15 \div 5 = 3$

DIVISION USING NUMBER LINE

Division can also be explained on the number line. Number line is a line on which numbers are given in an order.

Example 1: Show 6 ÷ 2 on the number line.

Solution: Start from 0 and jump 2 numbers every time till you reach 6. How many times did you jump?

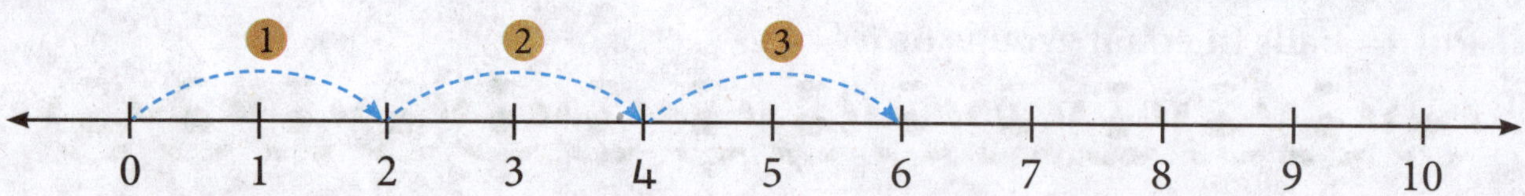

As you jumped 3 times to reach 6, the answer is 3. That is, $6 \div 2 = 3$

Example 2: Show 12 ÷ 3 on the number line.

Solution:

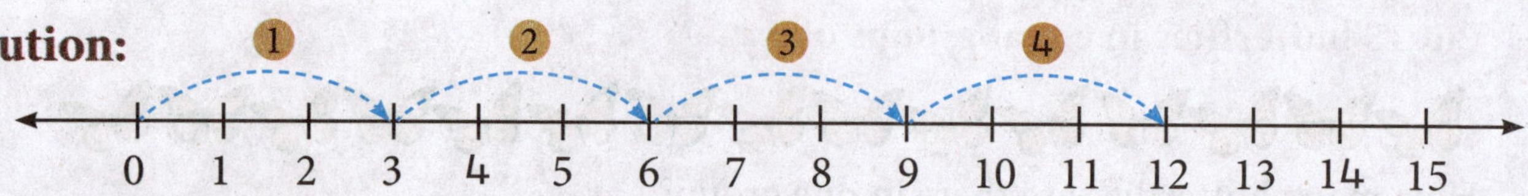

As there are 4 jumps from 0 to 12, the answer is 4. That is, $12 \div 3 = 4$

Mental Maths

Find out the answers through repeated subtraction.

1. 15 ÷ 3
2. 18 ÷ 9
3. 30 ÷ 10

EXERCISE 8B

1. **Solve the following using repeated subtraction. Write the division statements.**

   a. $50 \div 5 =$ ______ b. $48 \div 8 =$ ______ c. $63 \div 9 =$ ______ d. $16 \div 4 =$ ______

2. **Write the division statements for the following.**

   a. 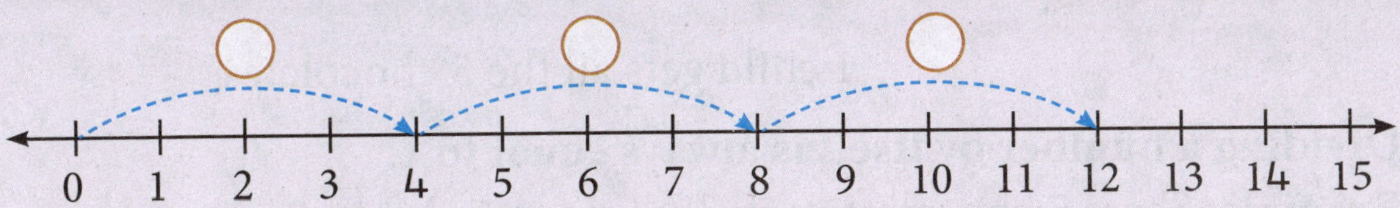

   b. 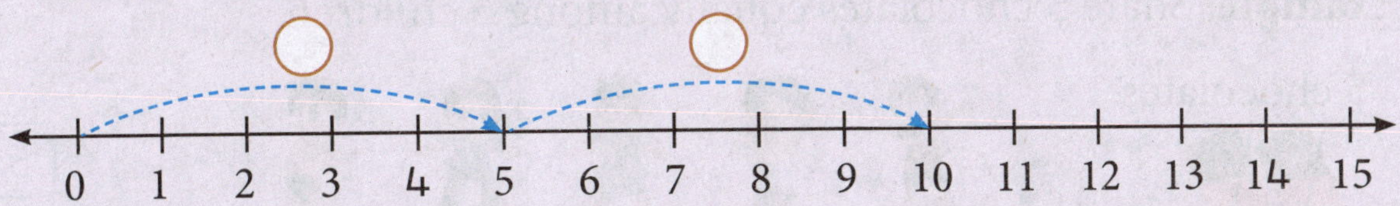

3. **Solve using number line.**

   a. $12 \div 2 =$ ______

   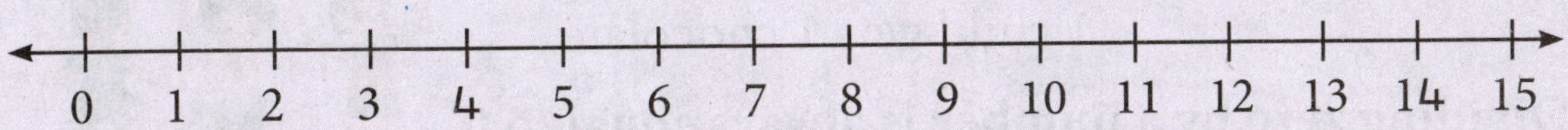

   b. $15 \div 3 =$ ______

   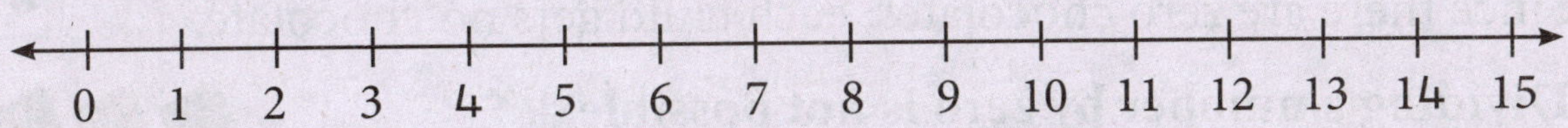

TERMS USED IN DIVISION

In a division statement, each number has a name. Consider the following division statement.

$10 \div 2 = \mathbf{5}$

10 is the dividend.
2 is the divisor.
5 is the quotient.

Dividend is the number which is being divided.

Divisor is the number which divides the dividend.

Quotient is the result of the division.

PROPERTIES OF DIVISION

1. Dividing a number by 1 is always equal to the number itself.

Example: Share 5 chocolates with 1 child.

$5 \div 1 = \mathbf{5}$

5 chocolates

1 child gets all the 5 chocolates.

2. Dividing a number by itself is always equal to 1.

Example: Share 5 chocolates equally among 5 children.

5 chocolates

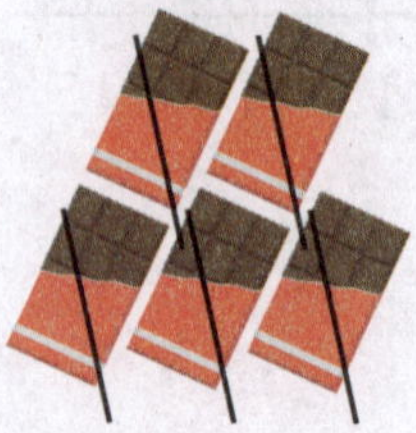

$5 \div 5 = \mathbf{1}$

1 child gets 1 chocolate.

3. Dividing zero by a number is always equal to 0.

Example: Share 0 chocolates equally among 5 children.

Since there are zero chocolates, each child gets no chocolate.

$0 \div 5 = \mathbf{0}$

4. Dividing a number by zero is not possible.

Example: Share 5 chocolates equally among zero children.

Since there are no children, it is not possible to do this division.

$5 \div 0 =$ Not possible

Go Easy!

If you remember the multiplication tables well, then division becomes easier.

Mental Maths

1. $25 \div 1 =$ ______
2. $17 \div 17 =$ ______
3. $0 \div 19 =$ ______

Note

There is a relationship between multiplication and division. Multiplication is the opposite of division. Division is the opposite of multiplication.

If $4 \times 2 = 8$, then $8 \div 4 = 2$ and $8 \div 2 = 4$.

Common Errors

$\frac{0}{5} = 5$ ✗ $\frac{0}{5} = 0$ ✓

$\frac{9}{0} = 0$ ✗ $\frac{9}{0} =$ Not Possible ✓

Maths Lab Activity

Aim: To reinforce the concept of division as equal grouping

Materials required: 15 marbles, 3 bowls

Procedure:

1. Take 15 marbles and 3 bowls.
2. Put one marble at a time in the 3 bowls till all the 15 marbles are put in them.
3. How many marbles do you manage to put in each bowl?

   15 marbles in 3 bowls can be placed one by one as shown.

   This can be written as $15 \div 3 = 5$.

   That is, 5 marbles are placed in each bowl.

Conclusion: Equal grouping means to make groups of items in such a way that each group has an equal number of items.

Concept Map

Introduction to division

- Division as equal sharing
- Division as equal grouping
- Division as repeated subtraction
- Division using number line
- Properties of division

Key Concepts

- **Division:** A method to share or group equally.
- **Equal sharing:** To distribute something in a way that it is shared equally
- **Equal grouping:** To make groups of items in such a way that each group has an equal number of items
- **Repeated subtraction:** It is another way to understand division where we subtract the same number many times from the total, till we get zero.
- **Number line:** A line in which numbers are given in an order
- **Dividend** is the number which is being divided. **Divisor** is the number which divides the dividend. **Quotient** is the result of division.
- Division by 1 is equal to the number itself. Division by the number itself gives 1. Dividing 0 by a number gives 0. Dividing a number by 0 is not possible.

Chapter Revision

A. Using equal grouping, fill in the blanks.

1. $6 \div 2 =$ _____ 
2. $8 \div 4 =$ _____ 
3. $10 \div 2 =$ _____ 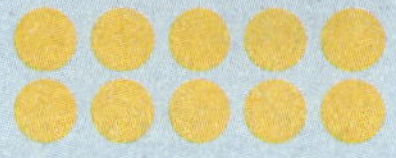
4. $12 \div 3 =$ _____ 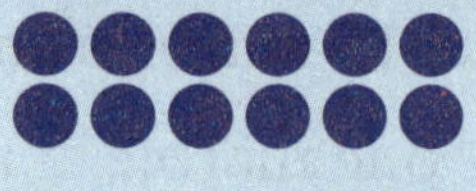
5. If $5 \times 2 = 10$, then $10 \div 5 =$ _____ and $10 \div 2 =$ _____

B. Write T for True and F for False.

1. $15 \div 5$ in repeated subtraction is 3. ☐

$$\begin{array}{r} 15 \\ -5 \;\; — \\ \hline 10 \\ -5 \;\; — \\ \hline 5 \\ -5 \;\; — \\ \hline 0 \\ \hline \end{array}$$

2. $16 \div 8$ as repeated subtraction is 2. ☐

$$\begin{array}{r} 16 \\ -8 \;\; — \\ \hline 8 \\ -8 \;\; — \\ \hline 0 \\ \hline \end{array}$$

3. a. $14 \div 7$ on the number line is 4. ☐

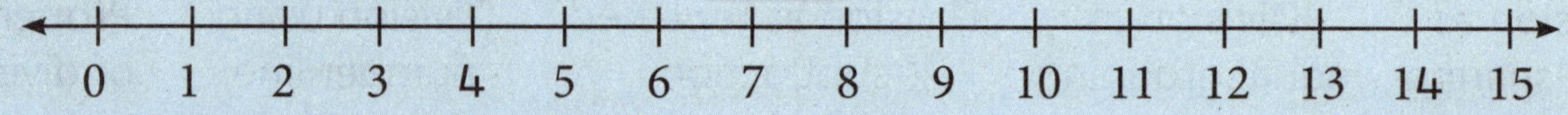

b. $10 \div 5$ on the number line is 2. ☐

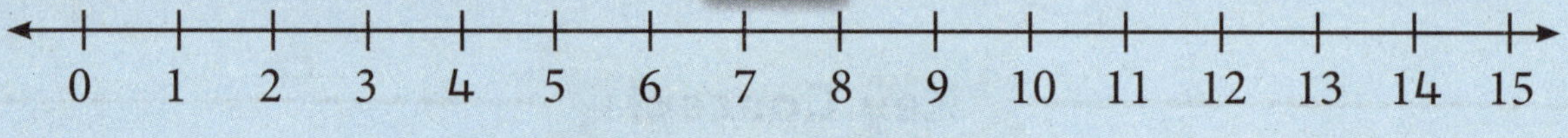

4. $8 \div 8 = 8$ ☐ 5. $0 \div 9 = 0$ ☐ 6. $10 \div 0 = 10$ ☐

C. Answer the following.

1. Aman wanted to colour 6 pages in 3 days.
   How many pages should he colour every day?

He should colour _____ pages every day.

2. Tarana wants to eat 10 apples in 5 days.
   How many apples should she eat every day?

She should eat _____ apples every day.

3. There are 35 packets of refreshments for a group of 5 friends. Find out how many packets can each friend get, if distributed equally.

SKILL UP!

Project

Try making the following equal groups of students in your class. How many groups do you make?

1. Take 6 students and make groups of 2 students each.

   Number of groups = ________________

   Therefore, $6 \div 2 =$ ________________

2. Take 15 students and make groups of 5 students each.

   Number of groups = ________________

   Therefore, $15 \div 5 =$ ________________

Life Skills

While playing a game, the teacher needed groups of 2 students each. There were 7 students. How many groups will be made?

We can make __________ groups and 1 child is left alone. Should we add one more child to make another group or should we let the seventh child be alone?

We should never let anyone feel left out!!

Mind Buzzer

If we arrange 9 marbles in groups of 2, how many groups do we get?

1. We get ________ groups and ________ extra marble.
2. If we want 5 groups, how many more marbles do we need? ________
3. If we want 6 groups, how many more marbles do we need? ________

Teacher's Notes

- The students can understand the concept of division very well if they make groups of items themselves.
- The students can practise making various groups with marbles, buttons or beans.
- They can also practise repeated subtraction with marbles, buttons or beans.

WORKSHEET

Meena is making five goody bags to give as return gifts on her birthday party. Help her to find out how many of each item she can put in one goody bag.

In each bag, she can put

1. __________ toffees
2. __________ chocolates
3. __________ stars
4. __________ crayon boxes
5. __________ sharpeners

9 Measurement

Learning Objectives

- To express and measure length in metres and centimetres
- To express and measure mass in kilograms and grams
- To express and measure capacity in litres and millilitres

Let's Get Started

1. Fill in the blanks using the correct option.
   a. The elephant is ________ than the zebra. (bigger/smaller)
   b. The monkey is ________ than the giraffe. (taller/shorter)
   c. The monkey is ________ than the elephant. (heavier/lighter)
2. The length of this pen = ________ paper clips.

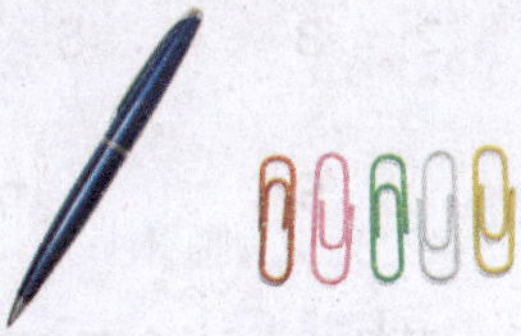

3. If the water of this jug is poured out, can it fill 3 glasses or 3 buckets.
   ________ (3 glasses/3 buckets)

MEASURING LENGTH

We learnt about uniform non-standard units of length in class 1. They are handspan, footspan, cubit or pace.

We also learnt to measure length using objects like paperclips, matchsticks, pens, erasers etc.

Metre and Centimetre

> **Note**
> Relationship between metre and centimetre
> **1 m = 100 cm**

To have an exact measurement of length instead of an estimation, standard units of measurement are used.

These are '**metre**' and '**centimetre**'.

We have fixed tools to measure the length of any object, like a ruler.

A **metre** is used to measure longer lengths. It is approximately equal to the distance, as shown, between both your hands if you stretch them.

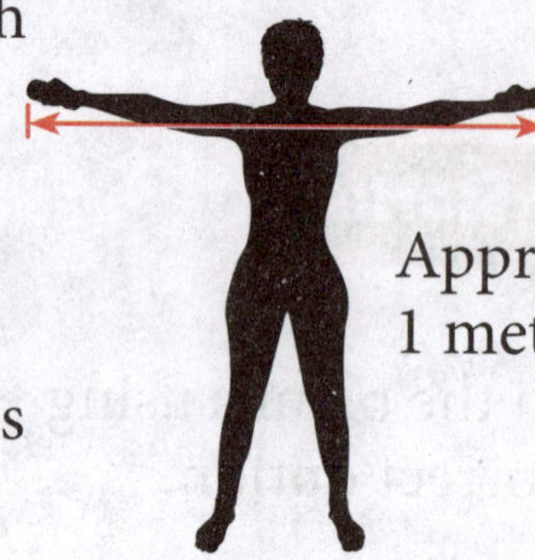

Approximately 1 metre

A metre is written as **m** in short form.

When you buy a piece of cloth, the shopkeeper measures it in metres.

A **centimetre** is used to measure shorter lengths. It is written as **cm** in short form.

Look at the ruler to see the length of a centimetre.

This length is equal to 1 cm.

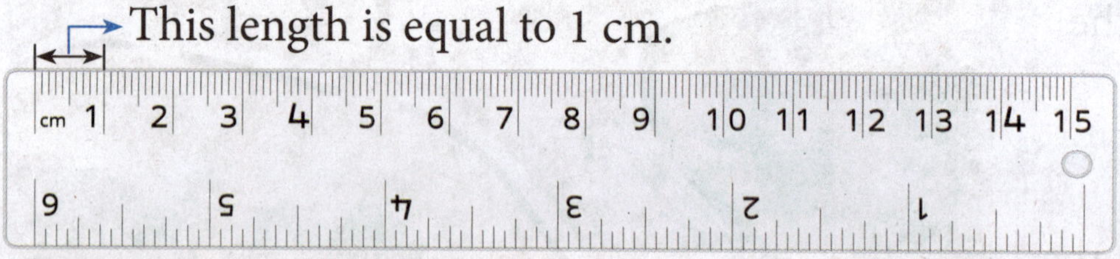

Let us measure the length of a few objects using a ruler.

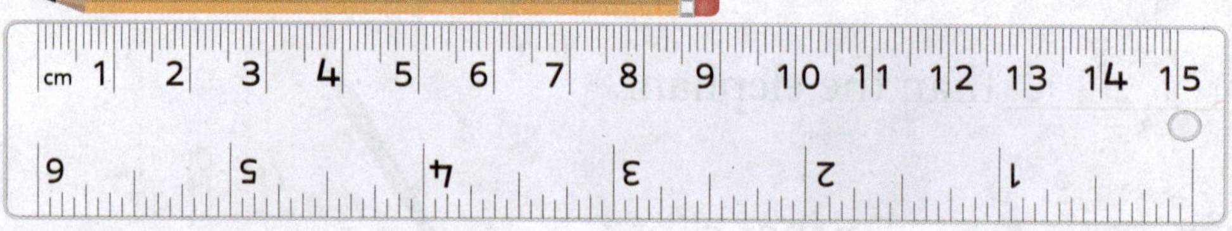

The length of the pencil is 9 cm.

> **Go Easy!**
> To measure the length of an object with a ruler, place the object at 0 cm at one end and note the measure on the ruler at another end of the object.

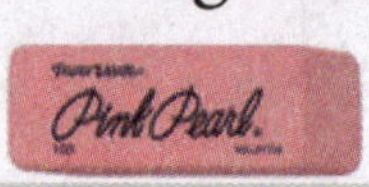

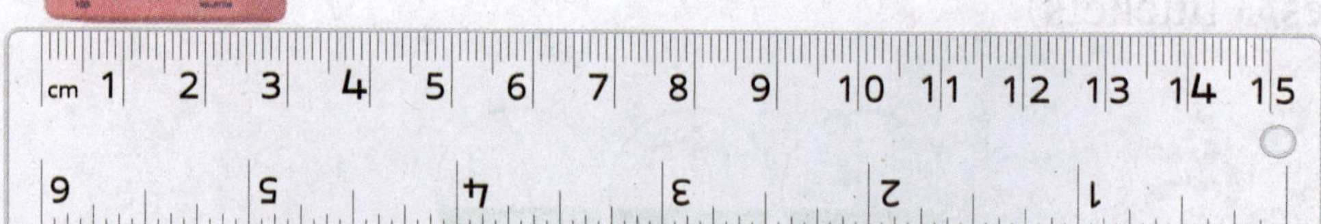

What is the length of this eraser? ☐ cm.

EXERCISE 9A

1. Which is a longer measurement – metre or centimetre? ____________

2. Circle the pictures which you think are less than 1 metre.

a. Length of train

b. Length of a pencil box

c. Height of a door

d. Length of a wallet

3. Circle the pictures which you think are more than 1 centimetre.

a. dot

b. Length of a pen

c. Length of a sharpener

d. Length of a shoe

4. Write which measurement (m or cm) can be used to measure the following.

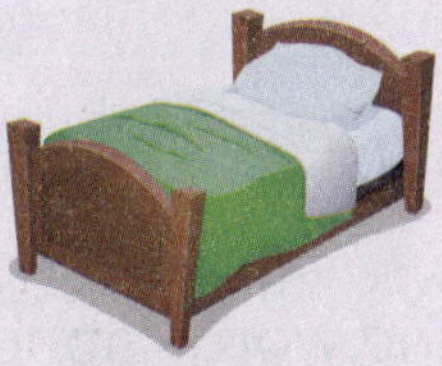
a. Length of bed ____________

b. Length of thumb ____________

c. Length of wall ____________

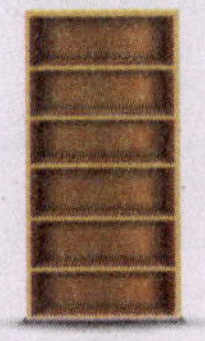
d. Length of big cupboard ____________

MEASURING MASS

Arijit could carry his school bag on his back but he could not pick up a larger suitcase.

That is because the larger suitcase is too heavy and the school bag is lighter in mass.

Weigh less than the glass

Weigh more than the glass

Try picking up various objects to see which is heavier and which is lighter.

Kilograms and Grams

Simple balance

We have learnt that the mass of an object can be measured using uniform non-standard units like stones, marbles, etc.

A simple balance or weighing balance is used to weigh things.

We use standard units like '**kilogram**' and '**gram**' to weigh objects.

Kilogram is written as '**kg**' in short form.

Gram is written as '**g**' in short form.

Kilograms are used to weigh heavier objects and grams are used to weigh lighter objects.

> **Note**
> Relationship between gram and kilogram
> **1 kg = 1000 g**

A teaspoon of salt weighs about 5 g.
A tablespoon of salt weighs about 15 g.

2 big pieces of ginger weigh about 100 g.
5 big pieces of ginger weigh about 250 g.

3 apples weigh about 500 g.
6 apples weigh about 1 kg.

> **Note**
> Why do we say the word, 'about' in measurement?
> It means that the measurement is not exact. It is an estimate.

EXERCISE 9B

1. How much would each object weigh? Tick (✔) the correct option.

a.  2 kg or 2 g ☐

b.  10 kg or 10 g ☐

c.  5 kg or 5 g ☐

d. 

100 kg or 100 g ☐

2. **Circle the objects which you think can weigh more than 1 kg.**

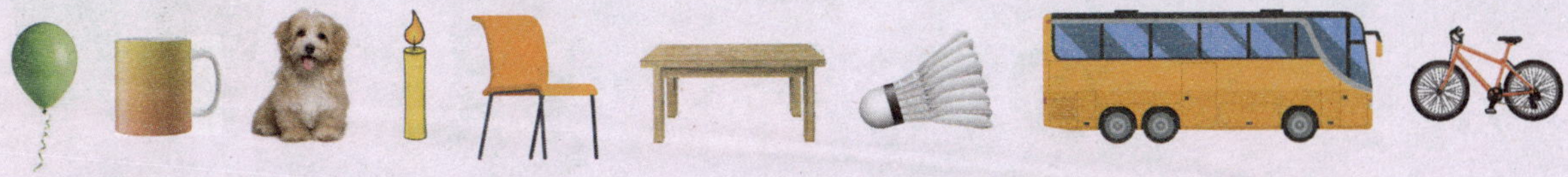

3. **Write how much would each of the following objects weigh. Fill in the blanks using: 500 g, 250 g, 1 kg, 100g**

a.

b.

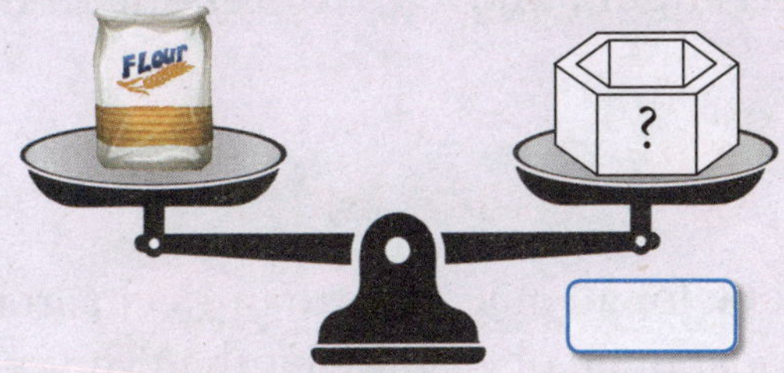

c.

d.

MEASURING CAPACITY

We know that the capacity of a container is equal to the amount of liquid that it can hold.

We have learnt to estimate and measure the capacities of containers using uniform non-standard units like cup, spoon, buckets, etc.

How many spoons of sugar will fill the bowl?

If 20 spoons of sugar fill the bowl, then we say that the capacity of the bowl is equal to 20 spoons.

Litres and Millilitres

We use the standard units '**litres**' and '**millilitres**' to measure capacity. **Litres** is written as 'ℓ' and **millilitres** is written as 'mℓ' in short forms.

> **Note**
> Relationship between litre and millilitre
> **1 ℓ = 1000 mℓ**

Millilitres are used to measure smaller quantities of liquid.

Litres are used to measure larger quantities of liquid.

1 teaspoon of liquid medicine is about 5 mℓ.

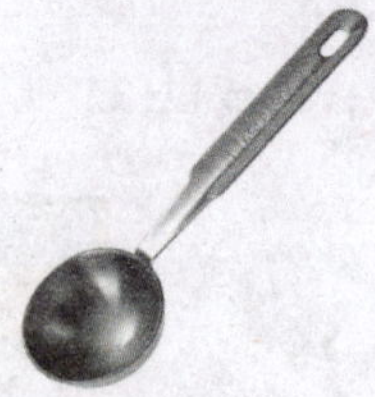

1 tablespoon of liquid medicine is about 15 mℓ.

A glass of water is about 200 mℓ.

A bucket of water is about 15 ℓ.

Mental Maths

Look for an object less than 15 cm around you.
Look for an object heavier than your pencil around you.

Do you know?

What do you think is the smallest measure of water that you might have seen?

A drop!

EXERCISE 9C

1. Tick (✔) the correct measurement.

a. 5 mℓ or 5 ℓ

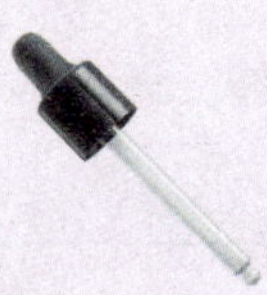

b. 1 mℓ or 1 ℓ

c. 250 mℓ or 250 ℓ

d. 20 mℓ or 20 ℓ

2. Tick (✔) the objects which can be measured in litres. Cross (✘) the objects which can be measured in millilitres.

a.  ☐

b.  ☐

c. 

☐

d. 

☐

e.  ☐

Go Easy!

Remember the units of measuring length, mass and capacity.

Length = m, cm   Mass = g, kg   Capacity = mℓ, ℓ

Maths Lab Activity

Aim: To reinforce the concept of capacity

Materials required: A jug and a glass

Procedure: Given that each glass of water measures 200 mℓ.

1. Take one glass of water at a time and pour it in a jug. Do this 5 times.
   200 mℓ + 200 mℓ + 200 mℓ + 200 mℓ + 200 mℓ
2. After addition, you will find that the jug now contains 1000 mℓ of water.
   5 glasses of water = 1000 mℓ, which is equal to 1 litre.
3. Observe and make a note of what would be the capacity of the jug.

Concept Map

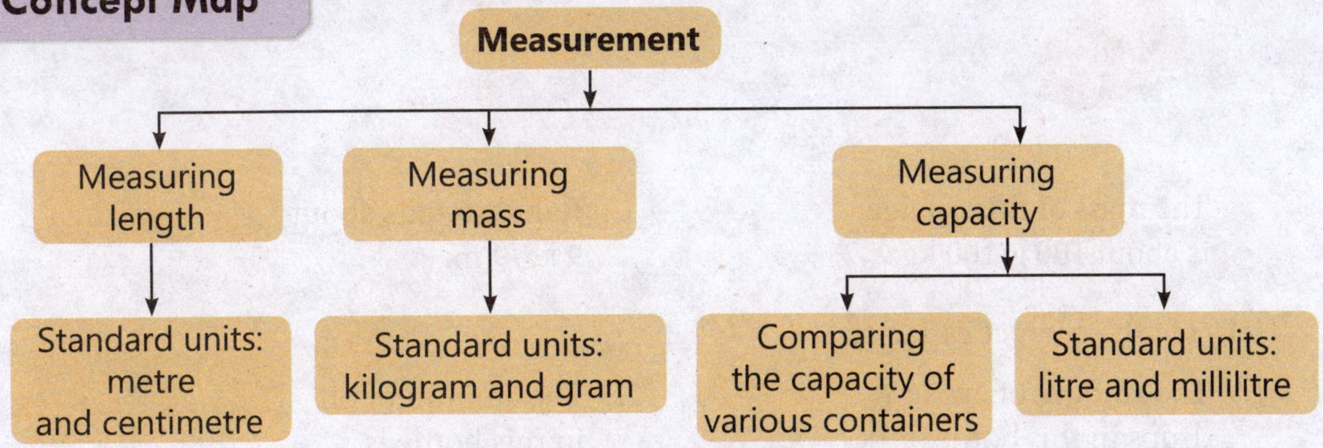

Key Concepts

- The standard units of measuring length are centimetre and metre.
- **Metre:** A unit of length to measure longer objects. Short form is 'm'.
- **Centimetre:** A unit of length to measure shorter objects. Short form is 'cm'.
- The standard units of measuring mass are gram and kilogram.
- **Kilogram:** A unit of mass to measure heavier objects. Short form is 'kg'.
- **Gram:** A unit of mass to measure lighter objects. Short form is 'g'.
- The standard units of measuring capacity are millilitre and litre.
- **Litre:** A unit of capacity to measure larger quantities of liquid. Short form is 'ℓ'.
- **Millilitre:** A unit of capacity to measure smaller quantities of liquid. Short form is 'mℓ'.

Chapter Revision

A. Tick (✔) the correct length.

1. 

The length of the sofa is about 2 cm/2 m.

2. 

The length of this wallet is about 7 cm/7 m.

B. How much will each of the following weigh? Tick (✔) the correct option.

1. 

The mass of this orange is about 100 g/100 kg.

2. 

Rahul weighs about 9 kg/9 m.

C. Tick (✔) the correct capacity.

1. The amount of eye drops in this bottle is about 20 mℓ/20 ℓ. 

2. The amount of oil in this bottle is about 5 mℓ/5 ℓ. 

D. Fill in the blanks.

1. The fixed units to measure length are _______ and _______. (ℓ, mℓ/m, cm)
2. The length of a register will be measured in _______. (m/cm)
3. Mass is measured in _______ and _______. (m, cm/g, kg)
4. Three onions will weigh in _______. (g, kg)
5. The capacity of a container is measured in _______. (ℓ/m)

E. Choose the correct option.

1. Metre measures a _______ (longer/shorter) length than centimetres.
2. Grams measure a _______ (lighter/heavier) mass than kilograms.
3. Litres measure a _______ (greater/smaller) capacity than millilitres.

SKILL UP!

Project

Pick up a few objects in your house and measure the length of each using a scale. A few examples are shown below.

1.  = _____ cm

2.  = _____ cm

3.  = _____ cm

4.  = _____ cm

Life Skills

Aditi filled 8 litres of water in a bucket. She used 6 litres to water the plants in the pots. She threw the rest of the water. How much water did she throw away? Is it fine to waste water?

Mind Buzzer

Fill a bucket with a mug and a jug. 12 jugs of water can fill the bucket.

If we try to fill the bucket with mugs, will it be more than 12 or less than 12 jugs? Why?

Teacher's Notes

- Let the students use rulers to measure certain objects. This would give them an idea of the measure of centimetre and metre.
- Make the students hold different objects in their hands to get an idea of how the things can weigh. Students can be taken to the labs, provided with some vegetables and asked to weigh them using a weighing balance for better understanding of grams and kilograms.
- The students can be asked to look for containers or bottles, bigger and smaller ones kept inside a refrigerator at home. This would help in understanding the concept of capacity.

WORKSHEET

Sachin, Anuj and Saif were running a race. Observe the picture and answer the following.

In 3 minutes, Sachin ran 95 metres. He drank 4 glasses of water after the race.

In 3 minutes, Anuj ran 89 metres. He drank 3 glasses of water after the race.

In 3 minutes, Saif ran 109 metres. He drank 1 glass of water after the race.

1. **Which child came first in the race? How many metres did he run in 3 minutes?**

   ____

2. **Which child drank the most water? How many glasses of water did he drink?**

   ____

3. **Arrange the names of the children in assending order of the metres covered by them in the race.**

   ____

4. **Tick (✓) the correct unit of measurement.**

   a. Mass of children

      g, kg

   b. Amount of water in one glass

      mℓ, ℓ

10 Shapes and Patterns

Learning Objectives

- To learn about different types of lines
- To learn about corners and edges
- To identify flat shapes and solid shapes
- To identify rolling and sliding objects
- To recognize different patterns based on shapes, numbers and letters

Let's Get Started

1. Colour the given shapes according to the colour codes.

Colour codes

- Blue
- Yellow
- Green
- Red

2. Match the shapes in Column A to the names in Column B.

Column A

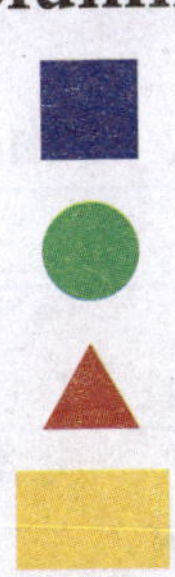

Column B

Triangle

Square

Rectangle

Circle

LINES

A line is a long mark that extends in both directions without any end. Lines can be straight or curved.

Go Easy!

The word 'Horizontal' starts with the letter H which has a line —— in the middle. This helps us to learn that Horizontal lines move from left to right like ——. The word 'Curve' starts with the letter C, which itself is a curve.

Straight Lines

Straight lines can move straight in any direction. They can be **vertical, horizontal** or **diagonal**.

Vertical lines	Horizontal lines	Diagonal lines
Also called standing lines.	Also called sleeping lines.	Also called slanting lines.
They move from top to bottom.	They move from left to right or right to left..	They can move in any direction.
The margin in your notebook is a vertical line.	The lines on which you write in your notebook are horizontal lines.	The rays of the sun are slanting lines.
Examples: 	**Examples:** 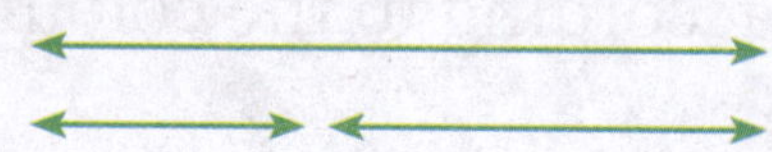	**Examples:** 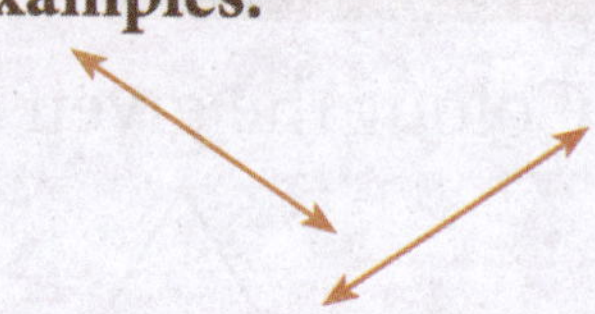

Curved Lines

If a line does not move straight and if it bends, then it becomes a **curved** line.

Examples:

A curved road looks like this.

EXERCISE 10A

Identify and mark the lines as V for vertical, H for horizontal, D for diagonal and C for curved.

WHAT ARE CORNERS AND EDGES?

Let us look at the following shapes.

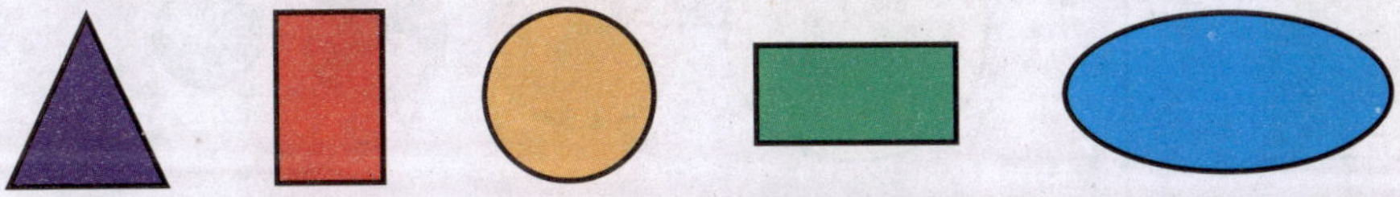

All these shapes are made up of curved lines and straight lines. These lines are called **sides** or **edges**.

Shapes with straight lines/edges	Shapes with curved lines/edges
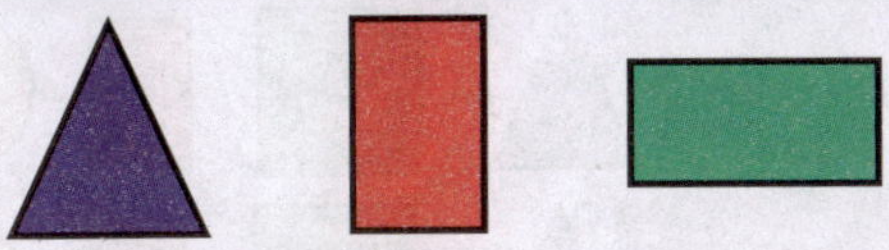	

Corners are the points where the edges meet.

FLAT SHAPES

Flat shapes are also called two-dimensional (2-D) shapes or plane shapes.

They can be made from lines or curves.

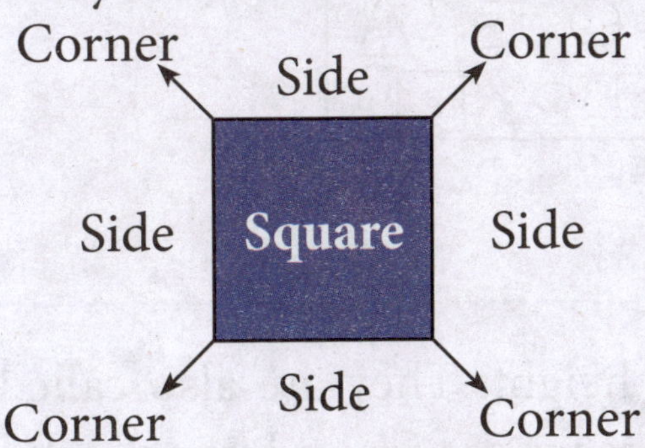

A square has 4 **edges and 4 corners.**

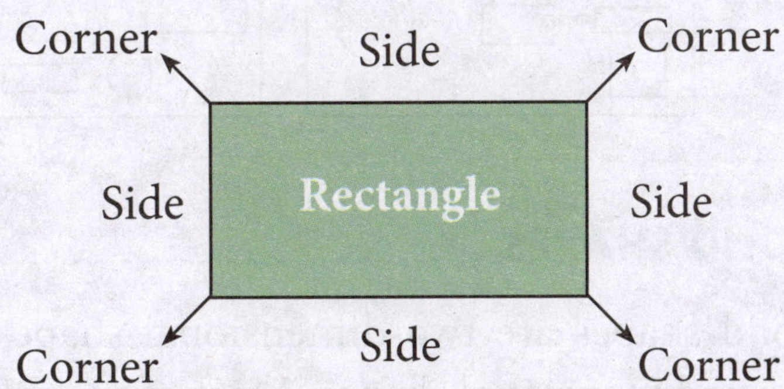

A rectangle has 4 **edges and 4 corners.**

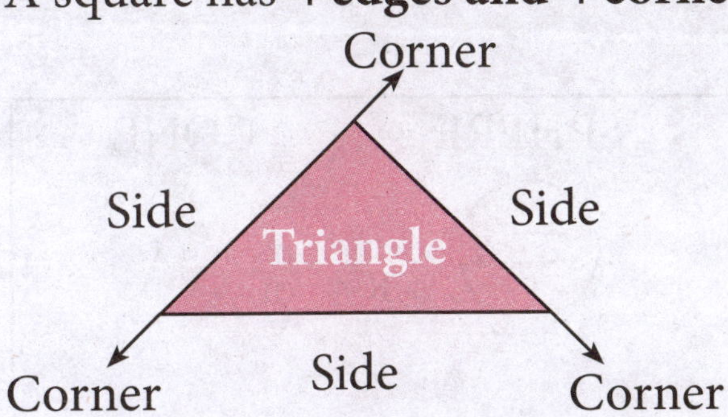

A triangle has **3 edges and 3 corners.**

Do you know?

TRI means 3. That is why a triangle has 3 sides.
Example: A tricycle has 3 wheels.

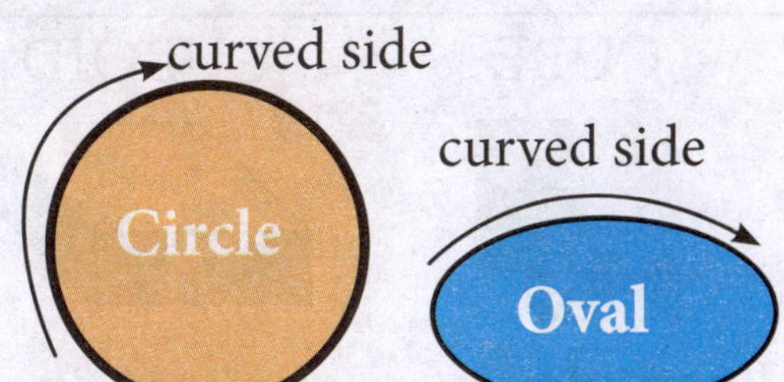

A circle is made up of a curve. There are **no straight lines or edges and no corners** in a circle. It has 1 curved side or curved edge.

Flat shapes can also be of different sizes as shown below.

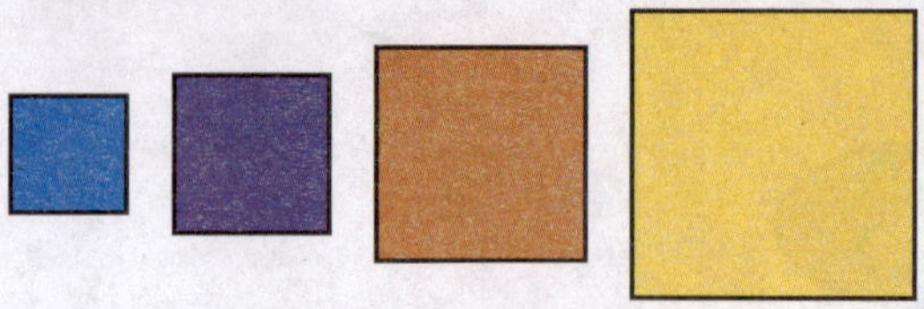

These are different sizes of square.

These are different sizes of circle.

EXERCISE 10B

1. **Circle the shapes which have 4 corners and 4 sides.**

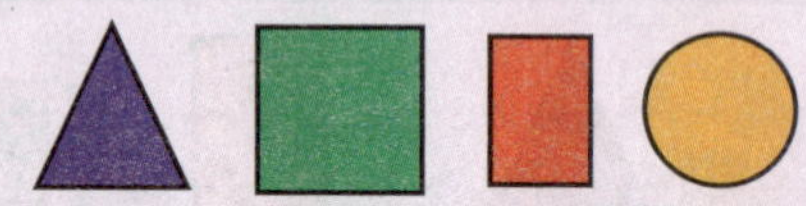

2. **Circle the shape which has no corners and no sides.**

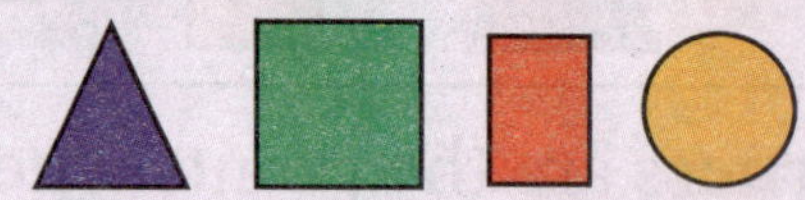

3. **Circle the shapes that are the same as the given coloured shape. Also, tick (✓) the shape that is the same size as the coloured shape given.**

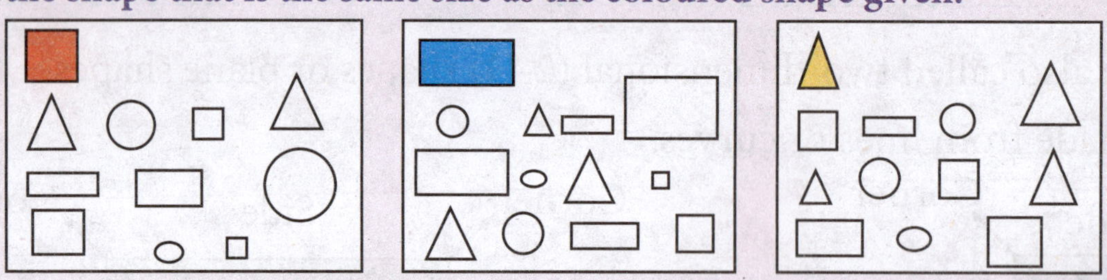

SOLID SHAPES

Solid shapes are two-dimensional shapes that have height. They are also called three-dimensional shapes. Most of the different shapes we see around us are solid shapes. Let us learn about some solid shapes.

CUBE	CUBOID	CYLINDER	SPHERE	CONE

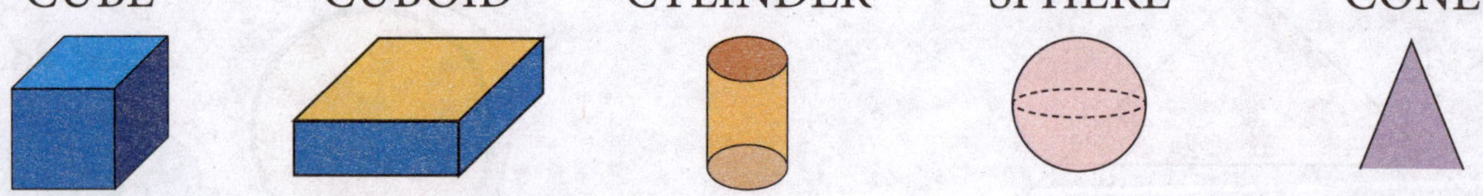

Examples:

Dice	Gift Box	Tin Can	Football	Party Cap

SOLID SHAPES AROUND US

When we look around us we can identify many objects which resemble some shapes. Let us take a look.

Shape	Objects
Cuboid	Building, Refrigerator
Sphere	Globe, Orange
Cube	Tissue box, Ice cube
Cylinder	Gas cylinder, Water bottle

ROLLING AND SLIDING OBJECTS

When a flat object is pushed, it slides. So, objects that have flat surfaces can slide.

When a curved object is pushed, it rolls. So, objects that have curved surfaces can roll.

Objects that have both flat and curved surfaces can slide as well as roll.

EXERCISE 10C

1. **Colour the pictures as per the given instructions.**

Colour the

Cuboids	–	Pink
Cubes	–	Blue
Spheres	–	Red
Cones	–	Purple
Cylinders	–	Green

2. **Look at the following things that you use at home and in school. Write down their names in the correct category.**

School bag

Battery cell

Eraser

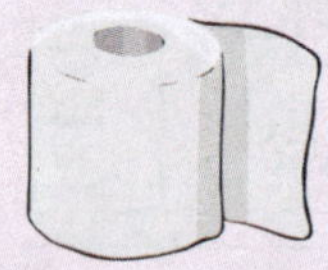
Tissue roll

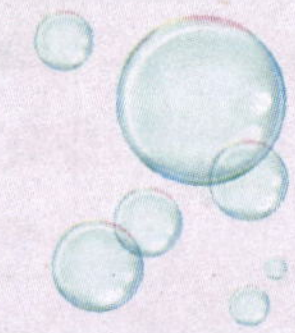
Water bubbles

Balloon

Cuboid	Cylinder	Sphere
____________	____________	____________
____________	____________	____________

3. **Write R for the objects that roll, S for the objects that slide and R and S for the objects that roll and slide.**

a.  ☐

b. 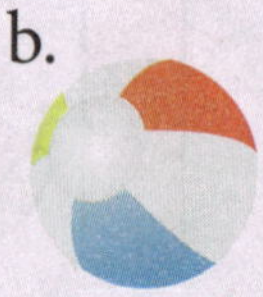 ☐

c.  ☐

d.  ☐

e.  ☐

f.  ☐

g.  ☐

h.  ☐

i.  ☐

PATTERNS

Patterns are a set of shapes, numbers or letters which repeat by following a certain rule or order. They help us to make beautiful decorations.

Examples:

Patterns in shapes

Patterns in letters and numbers

AB	BA	AB	BA	AB	BA
1	2	1	2	1	2

You can make patterns with your handprints and footprints too.

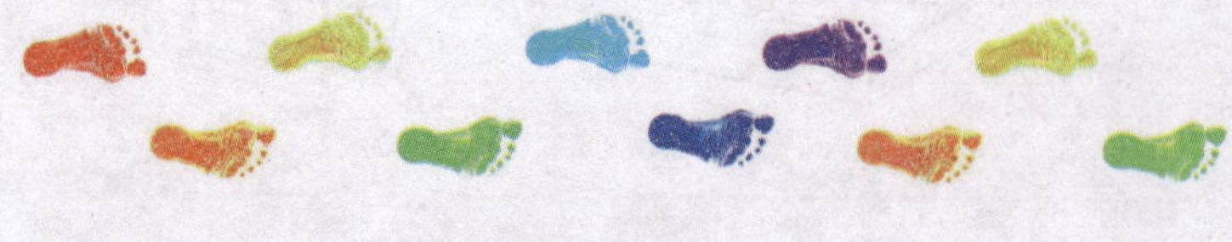

Patterns in Numbers

Observe the number patterns.

Rule: The number 2 is added each time.

Rule: The number 1 is subtracted each time.

EXERCISE 10D

Complete the following patterns.

1. 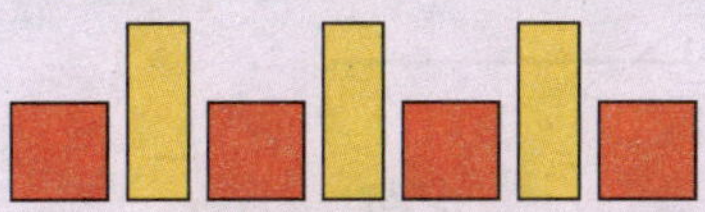 ______

2.  ______

3. 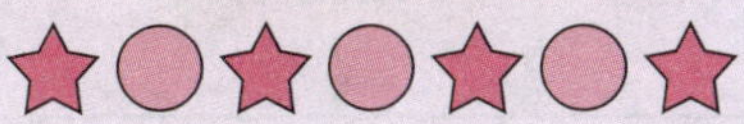 ______

4. 

5. 

4
______
______
______

6. 6, 8, 10, 12, _____, _____, _____ **Rule:** The number ___ is added each time.

PUZZLE!

How will you colour the grid given here with 4 colours of your choice to make a pattern.

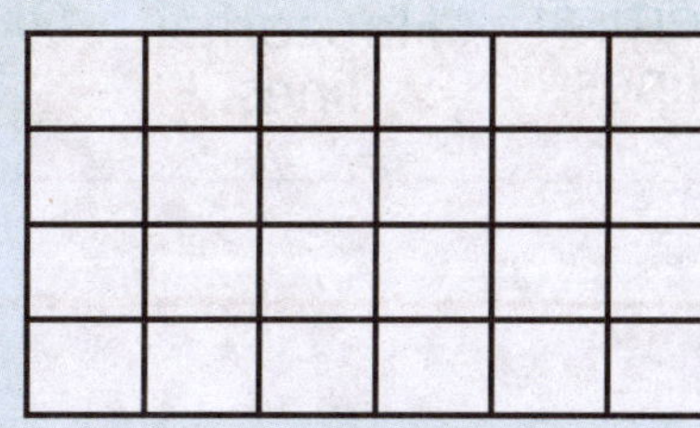

Mental Maths

1. The surface of a
   a. Cube is a ______ b. Cuboid is a ______ c. Cylinder is a ______ d. Cone is a ______
2. In a square, Number of sides = ________
3. In a triangle, Number of sides = ________ Number of corners = ________
4. In a rectangle, Number of sides = ________ Number of corners = ________
5. Which shape has no straight sides and no corners? ________

Maths Lab Activity

Aim: To make patterns from things around us

Materials required: Chart paper, colourful buttons, ribbons and some kitchen items

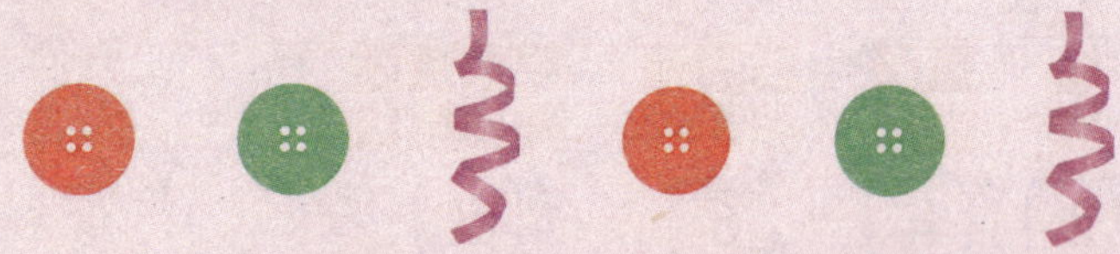

Procedure: 1. On a chart paper, stick a red button, then a green button and then a pink ribbon.

2. Repeat this pattern.
3. Similarly, make patterns using kitchen items like potatoes, onions, oranges and apples.

Concept Map

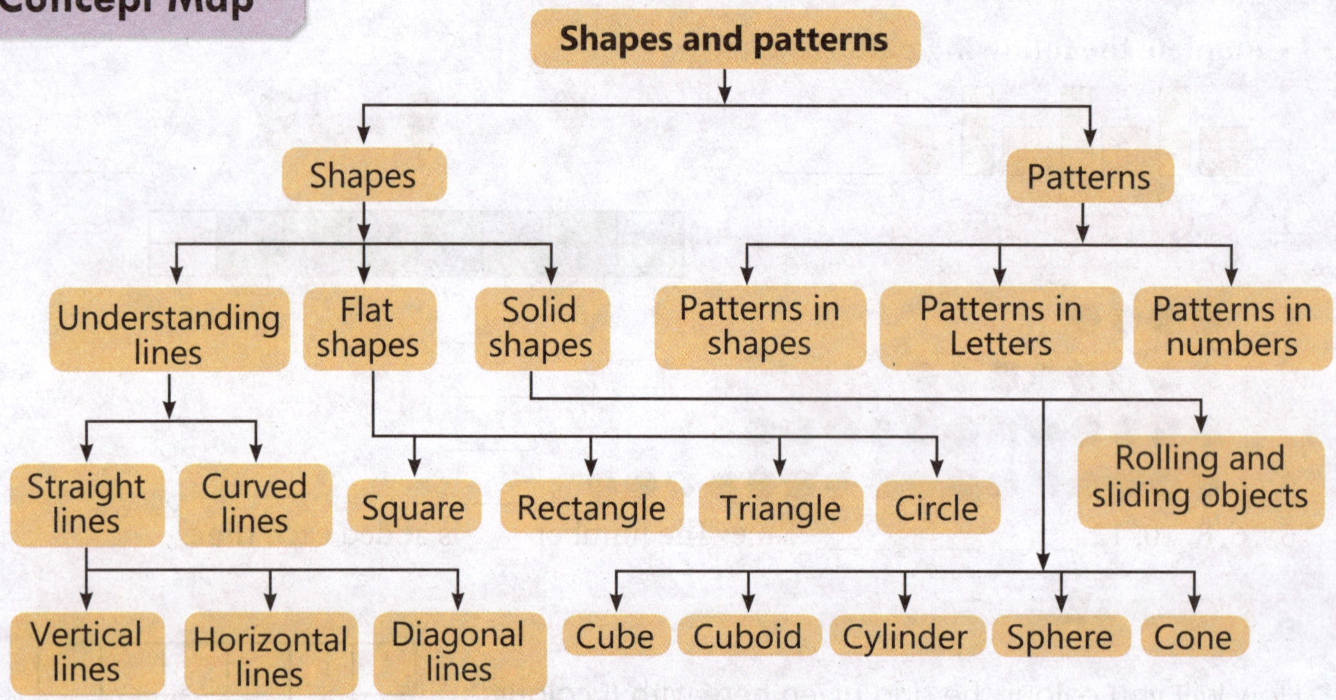

Key Concepts

- **Lines and curves:** Lines follow a straight path in a certain direction. Curves bend and do not follow a straight path.
- Shapes are made up of straight and curved lines called **edges**.
- **Corners** are the points where the edges meet.
- Square and rectangle have 4 edges and 4 corners. A triangle has 3 edges and 3 corners. A circle has no straight edges and no corners. It has one curved edge.
- **Flat shapes:** Flat shapes do not have height. They are also called two-dimensional shapes.
- **Solid shapes:** Solid shapes have height. They are also called three-dimensional shapes.
- **Rolling and sliding objects:** Objects that can roll or slide or both.
- **Patterns** exist in things around us; in shapes, numbers, colours, letters, etc.

Chapter Revision

A. Colour the shapes as per the colour codes.

Colour codes

- Square
- Rectangle
- Triangle
- Circle

Look at the red arrows marked here. Write:
V for vertical lines.
H for horizontal lines.
S for slanting lines.

B. These are items from Ms. Neera's kitchen. Write T for true and F for false.

Microwave

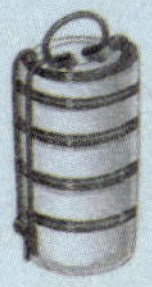
Lunch box

Bottle

Rolling pin

Ice cream

Orange

1. The lunch box has the shape of a sphere.
2. The strawberry ice cream is inside a brown coloured cone.
3. Another cone-shaped object is an orange.
4. The microwave has the shape of a cuboid.
5. There are three cylinder-shaped objects.

C Choose the correct option and circle it.

a. 

Cone
Cube
Cuboid

b. 
Sphere
Cube
Cone

c. 
Sphere
Cylinder
Cone

d. 
Cone
Sphere
Cylinder

e. 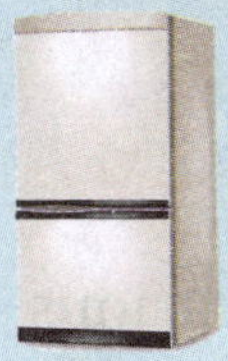
Cone
Cube
Cuboid

f. 
Cube
Sphere
Cuboid

D. Complete the patterns.

a.  ______, ______

b. 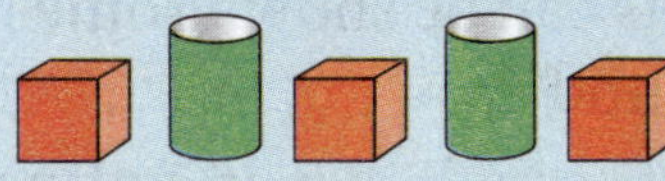 ______, ______

c. A, B, A, B, A, ______, ______

d. X, Y, Z, X, Y, Z, ______, ______, ______

e. 90, 80, 70, ______, ______, ______ **Rule:** The number ___ is subtracted each time.

SKILL UP!

Project

Take matchsticks and make shapes involving squares, rectangles and triangles.
Look at the example shown alongside.

Life Skills

Make a pattern with some students standing in a line holding hands.

Should we add another boy or a girl to complete the pattern?

If we do not complete the pattern, can the girl standing at the end feel left out?

Mind Buzzer

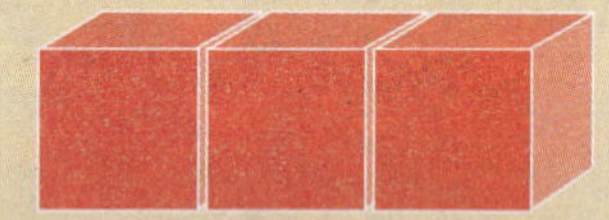

1. What happens when we combine two or more cubes?
   It becomes a ____________.
2. Which flat shape is used in the making of this toy box for kids? ______________________________

Teacher's Notes

- The students can be asked to identify the various kinds of lines around them in the classroom or surroundings.
- The students can be shown some flat and solid shapes in the form of wooden models or objects around us.
- The students can do paper cutting to make shapes.
- The students can practically roll and slide objects.

WORKSHEET

Colour the horse below using the colours of your choice to get beautiful patterns.

REASONING WORKSHEET 2

1. **Which product is the greatest?**

   a. 2×5 b. 2×4 c. 3×10 d. 5×7

2. **If one pencil costs ₹3, what will be the cost of two pencils? Tick (✓) the correct options.**

   a. ₹3 b. More than ₹3 c. Less than ₹3 d. ₹6

3. **If Samir wants to eat a pizza which has 8 slices in 4 days, how many slices should he eat equally every day?**

   a. 3 slices b. 4 slices

   c. 8 slices d. 2 slices

4. **If I can put 2 kg of flour in 1 jar, how many jars will I need for 4 kg of flour?**

   a. 3 jars b. 2 jars

   c. 1 jar d. 4 jars

5. **If I put two teaspoons of sugar in my tea, how many tablespoons will be needed to put the same quantity of sugar?**

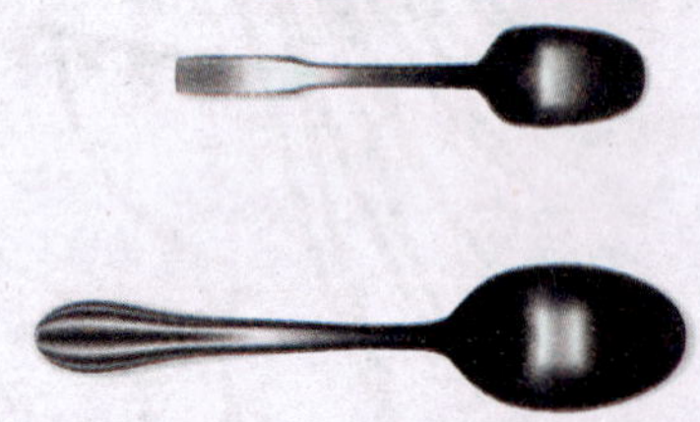

   a. More than 2 b. Less than 2

   c. More than half d. Equal to 2

6. **If all the sides of a rectangle are equal, it will become a:**

   a. Square b. Triangle c. Cuboid d. Cube

7. **If we join 2 cubes, it will become a:**

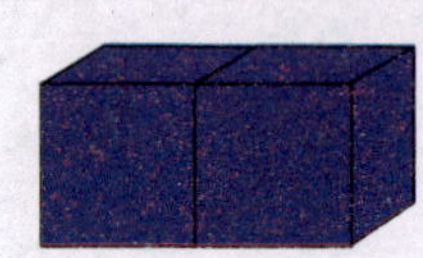

   a. Cube b. Square

   c. Rectangle d. Cuboid

8. **Which rule is followed in the number pattern formed by the cubes given below?**

   a. Start from 1 and add 2 every time

   b. Start from 1 and add 4 every time

   c. Start from 1 and add 3 every time

   d. Start from 1 and add 1 every time

11 Money

Learning Objectives

- To learn how to combine different notes and coins for given amounts
- To learn about Indian rupee and symbol
- To learn to add, subtract and compare different amounts of money
- To solve word problems on money

Let's Get Started

Pinky went to purchase a teddy bear, a doll and a frock. Calculate the amount of money spent on them as given below.

Note
The symbol '₹' is used to represent Rupee in India.

The cost of teddy bear is ₹ ______.

The cost of doll is ₹ ______.

The cost of frock is ₹ ______.

Money is needed to buy things. The currency used for money in India is **rupees**. We have notes and coins of different values. Every country has its own currency which is made of notes and coins.

> **Do you know?**
> Currency used in Japan is **Yen.**
> Currency used in Britain is **Pound.**
> Currency used in America is **US dollars.**
> Currency used in China is **Yuan.**
> Find out the currencies used in five other countries.

Indian Rupee

The Indian currency is called rupees and paise. The value of each note is written on both the sides. Following are some currency notes used in India.

> **Note**
> Rupees is also represented by **Rs.**

2 rupees

5 rupees

10 rupees

20 rupees

50 rupees

100 rupees

200 rupees

500 rupees

2000 rupees

In India, we use the following coins. The value of each coin is written only on one side.

25 paise

50 paise

1 rupee

2 rupees

5 rupees

10 rupees

ADDITION AND SUBTRACTION OF MONEY

When we go to a shop, we pay the shopkeeper for the things we buy. This often requires us to add or subtract money. Adding or subtracting money is just like adding or subtracting numbers.

> **Common Errors**
> Rs. 1 ✗ Re. 1 ✓
> For 1 rupee, we use Re.
> For more than 1 rupee, we use Rs.

Examples:

1. Find the total amount of money in each case.

a.  +  +  = ₹10 + ₹5 + ₹1 = ₹16

b.  +  + 

= ₹500 + ₹100 + ₹50 = ₹650

2. Subtract the following:

$= ₹50 - ₹20 = ₹30$

Comparing Money

We can compare the amounts of money using >, < or =.

Arya bought a video game for

= ₹650

Naina bought another video game for

= ₹610

Whose video game was cheaper comparatively?

As 610 < 650, Naina's video game was comparatively cheaper.

EXERCISE 11A

1. Find the total amount of money in each case.

a.  = ₹____

b.  = ₹____

c.  = ₹____

d.  = ₹____

2. Compare the amounts of money using >, < or = .

a.  ☐ 

b.  ☐ 

c.  ☐ 

d.  ☐ 

WORD PROBLEMS

Example 1: Samira bought a dress for ₹250 and a pair of shoes for ₹125. How much money did she spend?

Solution: Cost of dress = 2 5 0

Cost of shoes = + 1 2 5

3 7 5

She spent ₹375.

Example 2: A book costs ₹395. A pen costs ₹75. How much more does the book cost than the pen?

Solution: Cost of book = 3 9 5

Cost of pen = − 7 5

3 2 0

The book costs ₹320 more than the pen.

EXERCISE 11B

1. **A shirt costs ₹520 and a book costs ₹270. How much do both the things cost?**

   Both the things cost ₹__________.

2. **Ehbok has ₹990. Rajesh has ₹870. How much more money does Ehbok have than Rajesh?**

   Ehbok has ₹__________ more than Rajesh.

3. **I want to buy a toy aeroplane for ₹330. If I give the shopkeeper ₹350, how much money will he return?**

   The shopkeeper will return ₹__________.

4. **Two children save money for watching a movie. Each movie ticket costs ₹440. How much money will they need to collect?**

   They collect ₹__________.

Go Easy!

To add different amounts of money, start counting from the greatest amount.

Example: Here we are given some amounts of notes and coins. We will start counting from ₹500 note, then ₹100 note, ₹50 note and then the ₹10 coin, for making calculations simpler.

Mental Maths

1. If Radhika saves ₹100 every month. How much money will she save in 6 months? ₹__________
2. Kapil and Sunil both have ₹200 each. What is the total amount of money they have altogether? ₹__________
3.  +  +  +  = ₹__________

Maths Lab Activity

Aim: To understand addition, subtraction and comparison of money

Materials required: Toys of various kinds like dolls, teddy bears, aeroplane, etc.

Procedure: It is 'Toy Day' in school.

1. Arrange the classroom into 2 groups - Group A and Group B
2. Let Group A be a team of sellers. Let Group B be a team of buyers.
3. Some of the toys for sale by Group A are given.

₹330	₹75	₹50	₹150	₹200

   a. Nick is a buyer from Group B. He wishes to buy a ball and a car. How much money will he have to spend? ₹__________.
   b. Nina wants to buy a toy that is the cheapest. Which toy would she be able to buy?
   c. Buying a teddy bear and a doll is costlier than buying a ball and an aeroplane. True or False. __________
   d. Give a combination of notes or coins that can be used by Nick and Nina to buy the toys that they wish to buy?

Combination of notes and coins

Concept Map

Money

- Making combinations of rupees and coins
- Adding the amounts of money
- Subtracting the amounts of money
- Word problems
  - find the cost
  - how much money

Key Concepts

- **Money** is available in the form of currency notes and coins.
- **Currency** is a term used to represent money. Indian currency is **rupees**.
- ₹ is the symbol of Indian rupees.
- Adding, subtracting and comparing money in real life by solving word problems.

Chapter Revision

A. Fill in the blanks using >, < or =.

1.  +  ☐ 

2.  ☐  +  + 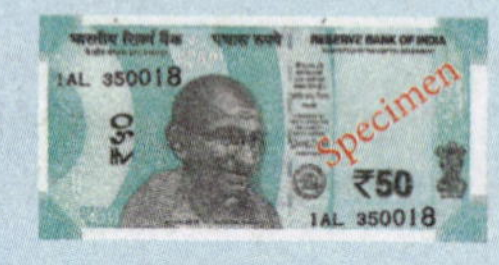

B. Find the total amount of money in each case.

1.  +  + 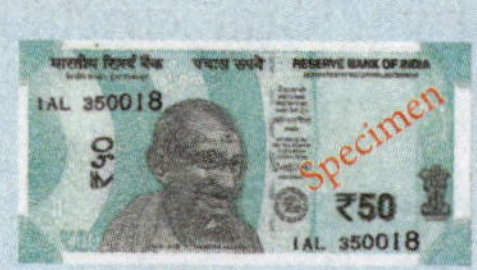 = ₹______

2.  +  +  = ₹______

C. Answer the following.

1. Anil has ₹240 and Sunil has ₹510. How much money do they have altogether?
   Together, they both have ₹____________.
2. A shirt costs ₹250. How much will 2 such shirts cost?
   2 such shirts will cost ₹____________.
3. A chair costs ₹659. A lamp costs ₹445. How much more does the chair cost than the lamp?
   The chair costs ___________ more than the lamp.

4. Neena has ₹97 in her wallet. She decided to buy an ice cream for ₹35. How much money is left with her? Express the left amount in a combination of notes and coins in the space provided.

Combination of notes and coins

SKILL UP!

Project

The students can work in groups to make ten different combinations of ₹100 using the following sets of combinations of notes and coins.

1. 4 notes of 20
2. 4 notes of 10
3. 6 notes of 5
4. 10 coins of 2
5. 10 coins of 1

Life Skills

Megha, Radha and Sneha went to buy some doughnuts. Megha had ₹50. Radha had ₹60 and Sneha had ₹45. The cost of one doughnut is ₹50.

1. Who will be able to buy the doughnut? ______________________
2. Do you think Sneha will be able to buy a doughnut? ______________________
3. How much more money she needs to buy a doughnut? ₹______________________.
4. Can Megha or Radha help Sneha to buy a doughnut? ______________________
5. Who can help her? ______________________
6. Do you think we should help people in need? ______________________

Mind Buzzer

Pinky went to a salon for haircut and head massage. The cost of haircut service is ₹450. The cost of head massage service is ₹200.

Pinky has ₹600 in her wallet. Will she be able to take both the services?

Teacher's Notes

- Dummy currencies can be brought to class to help students identify the notes and coins properly.
- Set up a real-life scenario like buying–selling sessions in classroom for them to understand how to buy things and add and subtract money.
- Activities can be conducted that help students learn how to save money and spend it wisely rather than lavishly.

WORKSHEET

A. Given below are some stationery items bought by Geeta. Complete the bill.

Item	Cost per item	Price (in ₹)
1 pen	20	20
2 pencils	15	
3 erasers	10	
2 rulers	20	
1 pencil box	35	
Total		

B. Tick (✔) the currency note or notes that can be given to the shopkeeper by Geeta to buy the items.

12 Time

Learning Objectives

- To read and write the time to half past the hour
- To learn about the days of the week and months of the year
- To learn about the sequence of seasons in the year

Let's Get Started

We learnt about the minute hand and the hour hand in class 1.

The long hand is the minute hand.

The short hand is the hour hand.

The activities in a school are scheduled as given below.

Prayer time (7:00)	Physical training (9:00)	Break (11:00)	Dance class (1:00)
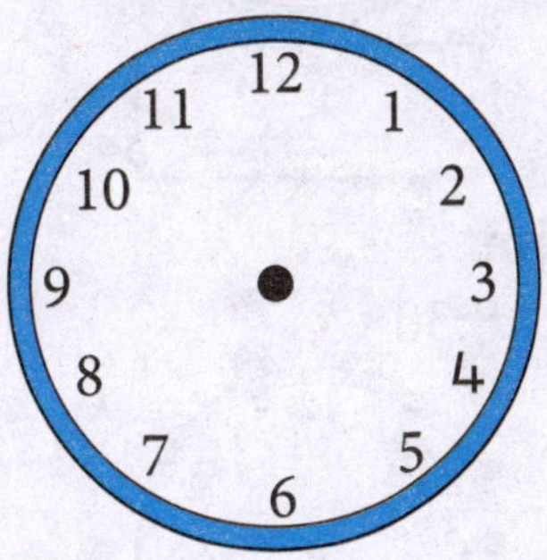	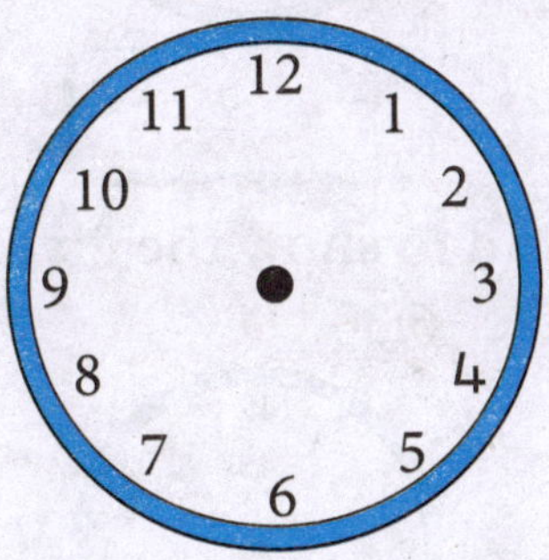	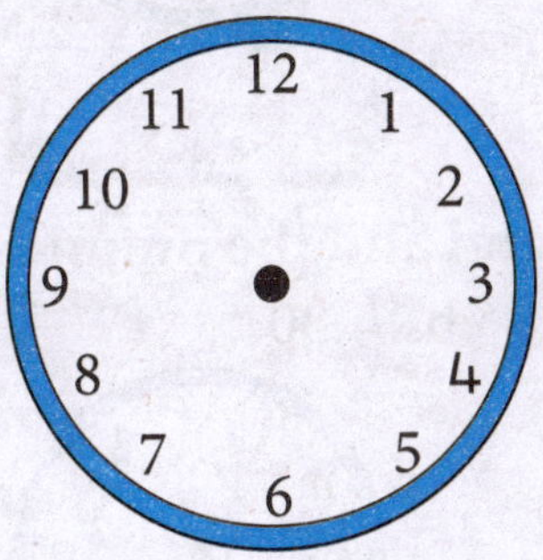	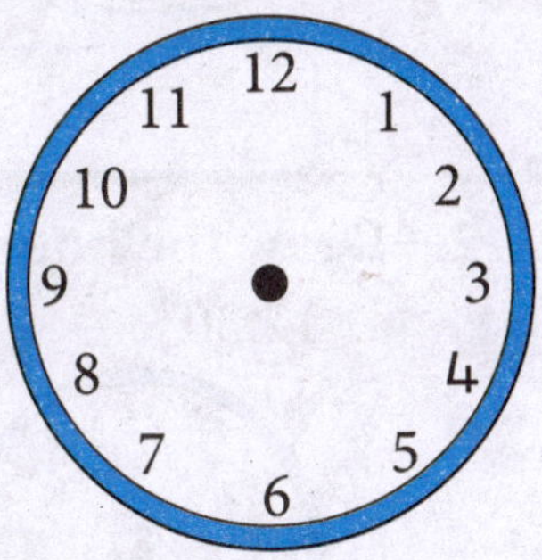

Draw the hands of the clock to show the given time.

READING TIME TO HALF PAST THE HOUR

We know that a clock tells us exactly what time of the day it is.

The minute hand takes one hour to go around the clock.

In this one hour, the hour hand goes from one number to the next.

If the minute hand starts from 12, goes around the clock from the right side and reaches 12 again, it means one hour is completed.

Note
The minute hand moves faster than the hour hand.

If the minute hand starts from 12 and reaches 6, it means half an hour is completed.

The minute hand is at 6.
The hour hand is in between 2 and 3.
It is read as **half past two** or two-thirty.
It is written as 2:30.

The minute hand is at 6.
The hour hand is in between 5 and 6.
It is read as **half past five** or five-thirty.
It is written as 5:30.

The minute hand is at 6.
The hour hand is in between 10 and 11.
It is read as **half past ten** or ten-thirty.
It is written as 10:30.

EXERCISE 12A

Common Errors
6.30 ✗ 6:30 ✓

1. **Write the time shown in the clocks.**

a. 

b. 

c. 

d. 

2. **Draw the hour hand and the minute hand to show the given time.**

a. 12:30 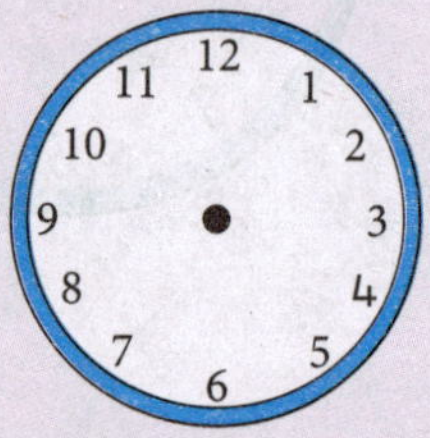

b. 4:30 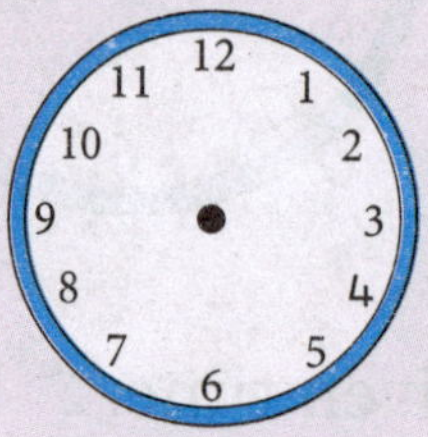

c. 6:30 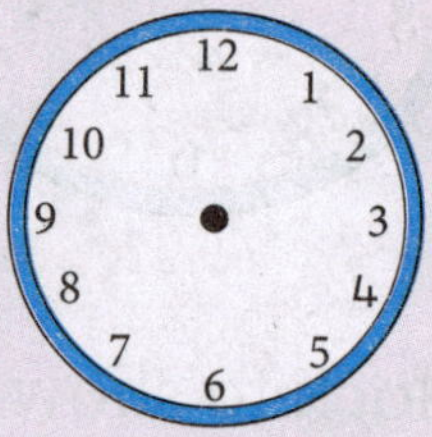

d. 8:30 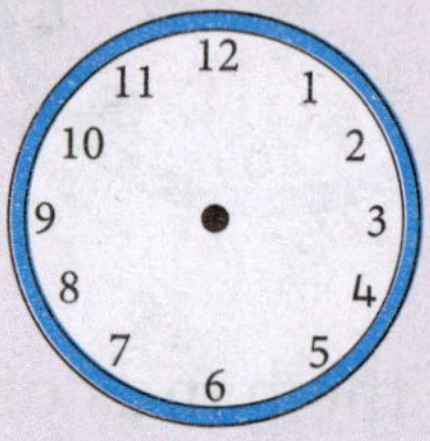

3. **Given below is the school time table of class 2.**

Answer the following.

a. The students reached the school at __________.

b. The teacher teaches the class at __________.

c. The students have lunch together during the breaktime at __________.

d. The students get half an hour break to play at __________.
When will the breaktime get over? __________.

e. The students reach home and meet their mother at __________.

DAYS OF A WEEK

There are seven days in a week. Let us look at the order of these days.

Days of the week	Monday	Tuesday	Wednesday	Thursday	Friday	Saturday	Sunday
Order of Days	First	Second	Third	Fourth	Fifth	Sixth	Seventh

Sam and Rohan are school friends. John and Neha are siblings.

Monday	Wednesday	Thursday	Friday	Sunday
 Sam	 Rohan	 John	 Neha	 John and Neha

a. Who went to school on Monday? ________

b. Which day did the siblings go for cycling? ________

c. Neha studied for her exam on ________.

d. Rohan felt sick and went to the doctor on ________.

e. ________ is seen to be swimming. Which day of the week is it? ________.

Yesterday, Today and Tomorrow

We all know that today is the present day.

If today is Saturday, then the day before was Friday and the day after will be a Sunday.

The day before is called **yesterday**.

The day after is called **tomorrow**.

Friday (Yesterday)	Saturday (Today)	Sunday (Tomorrow)

So, if today is Saturday, then yesterday was Friday and tomorrow will be Sunday.

EXERCISE 12B

1. Match the following.

a. Number of days in a week	Saturday
b. The day just after Tuesday	Tuesday
c. This day comes just before Sunday	Friday
d. Yesterday was Monday, then today is	Seven
e. Today is Thursday, then tomorrow will be	Wednesday

2. Fill in the blanks.

a. __________ is the last day of the week.

b. __________ is two days before Thursday.

c. __________ is the fourth day of the week.

d. Tomorrow will be __________, if today is Saturday.

3. Pinky's class test took place on Monday. Her teacher announced the results two days after the test. Which day did the students get their results?

____

Mental Maths

1. Tomorrow will be ____________, if yesterday was Monday.
2. If today is Monday, then the day after tomorrow will be ____________.
3. The fifth day of the week is __________.
4. The number of days in 3 weeks is __________.
5. 7:30 is read as __________ or __________.

MONTHS OF THE YEAR

There are 12 months in a year. Let us look at their order and the number of days in each month.

Months	Order	Number of Days
JANUARY	First	31
FEBRUARY	Second	28 or 29
MARCH	Third	31
APRIL	Fourth	30
MAY	Fifth	31
JUNE	Sixth	30
JULY	Seventh	31
AUGUST	Eighth	31
SEPTEMBER	Ninth	30
OCTOBER	Tenth	31
NOVEMBER	Eleventh	30
DECEMBER	Twelfth	31

A year has 365 days.

Mental Maths

1. Which two consecutive months have 31 days?
2. The only month which does not have 30 or 31 days is __________.

Note

1. February has 28 days. But it has 29 days which occurs every 4 years. It is the shortest month of the year.
2. Months have 30 or 31 days alternatively.
3. Leap year is the year which has 366 days. February has 29 days in a leap year.

Go Easy!

Let us learn the names of 12 months using our fist.

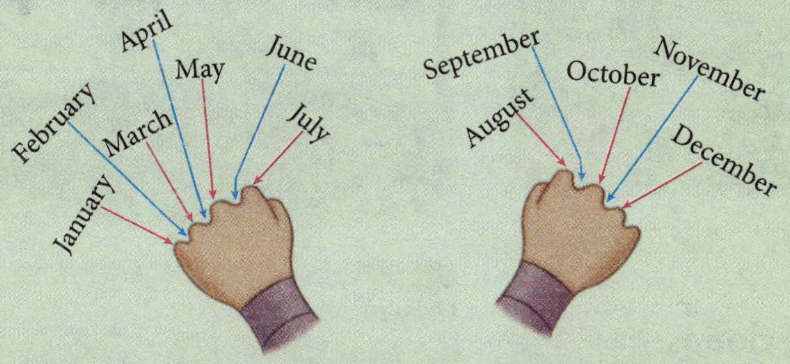

Learn the months by counting them on the knuckles and the grooves between the knuckles. Do not count the thumb knuckle.

The months counted on the knuckle have 31 days and the months counted on the grooves have 30 days (28 or 29 days for February).

Do you know?

July was named after Julius Caesar, the Roman Politician and Military General.

Augustus Caesar was grandnephew of Julius Caesar who came into power after Julius and the month of August was named after him.

SEASONS OF THE YEAR

There are five seasons in a year. Let us learn about them.

Winter

It is a very cold season. Snowfall happens in some areas during this season. People usually wear jackets, sweaters and other woollen clothes.

Spring

Spring comes after winter. New plants grow, flowers blossom and new leaves grow in spring. Weather starts to warm up.

Summer

It is a very hot season. Summer season comes after spring season. People usually wear cotton clothes.

Monsoon (Rainy)

Sky gets covered with dark clouds. It rains with thunderstorms. Surroundings get wet and cools the atmosphere. People wear raincoats and use umbrellas. A rainbow is seen sometimes when the rain stops.

Autumn

It is a pleasant season. The leaves change colour. They start falling from trees so that new leaves can come in spring. Autumn comes before winter.

EXERCISE 12C

1. Match the following.

a. The third month of the year	November
b. The month just before August	June
c. The month not having 30 or 31 days	July
d. December comes after this month	February
e. The sixth month of the year	March

2. Fill in the blanks.

a. Months that have 30 days are ____________________

b. Name your birthday month? ____________. Which day is it in the present year? ____________

c. Trees shed their leaves in ____________ season.

d. The season in which people usually wear cotton clothes is __________.

e. People wear sweaters and jackets in ________ season.

f. The weather in autumn is ____________.

g. People wear raincoats in ____________ season.

3. Name the following seasons.

a. Hot season ________

b. Pleasant season ________

c. Cold season ________

d. New leaves come in this season ________

e. Wet surroundings ________

CROSSWORD

Fill in the crossword given below after studying the clues given.

Across

1. The long hand of a clock is called the ________ hand.
2. The month after May
3. The month after March
5. The day after today

Down

1. The first day of the week
2. The day after Wednesday
3. 10:30 is read as ________ past 10.
4. The season when we feel very hot

Maths Lab Activity

Aim: To identify the days and months of the year

Materials required: A calendar

Procedure:

1. Think of special holidays in a year like
   Republic Day,
   Independence Day,
   Mahatma Gandhi's birthday,
   Children's Day,
   Christmas and
   New Year's Day
2. Mark all the above holidays in the calendar.
3. Write the day on which each of them will fall in the space given below.

Republic Day	________	Independence Day	________
Mahatma Gandhi's birthday	________	Children's Day	________
Christmas	________	New Year's Day	________

Concept Map

Time

- Read and write time to half past the hour

- **Days of the week**
  Monday, Tuesday, Wednesday, Thursday, Friday, Saturday, Sunday
- **Months of the year**
  January, February, March
  April, May, June
  July, August, September
  October, November, December
- **Seasons**
  Winter
  Spring
  Summer
  Monsoon
  Autumn

Key Concepts

- When the minute hand starts from 12 and reaches 6, it completes half past the hour.
- There are 7 days in a week.
- There are 12 months in a year. February has 28 days.
- A year has 365 days and a leap has 366 days.
- February has 29 days in a leap year.
- There are 5 seasons in a year.

Chapter Revision

A. Fill in the blanks.

a. Half past 11 is written as ______________. (11:00/11:30)

b. There are ______________ days in a week. (7/8)

c. If yesterday was Thursday, then today is ______________. (Wednesday/Friday)

d. Flowers bloom in the ______________ season. (Spring/Winter)

B. Draw the hour hand of the clock to show the given time.

a. 7:30

b. 11:30

c. 9:30

d. 3:30

C. Write T for true and F for false.

a. When the minute hand goes around the clock from 12 to 5, half an hour is completed. ☐

b. Three days after Wednesday is Saturday. ☐

c. Monday is the last day of the week. ☐

d. Thursday comes after Tuesday. ☐

e. There are 30 days in February. ☐

D. Look at the 2021 calendar below and answer the following.

2021

JANUARY

Mo	Tu	We	Th	Fr	Sa	Su
				1	2	3
4	5	6	7	8	9	10
11	12	13	14	15	16	17
18	19	20	21	22	23	24
25	26	27	28	29	30	31

FEBRUARY

Mo	Tu	We	Th	Fr	Sa	Su
1	2	3	4	5	6	7
8	9	10	11	12	13	14
15	16	17	18	19	20	21
22	23	24	25	26	27	28

MARCH

Mo	Tu	We	Th	Fr	Sa	Su
1	2	3	4	5	6	7
8	9	10	11	12	13	14
15	16	17	18	19	20	21
22	23	24	25	26	27	28
29	30	31				

APRIL

Mo	Tu	We	Th	Fr	Sa	Su
			1	2	3	4
5	6	7	8	9	10	11
12	13	14	15	16	17	18
19	20	21	22	23	24	25
26	27	28	29	30		

MAY

Mo	Tu	We	Th	Fr	Sa	Su
					1	2
3	4	5	6	7	8	9
10	11	12	13	14	15	16
17	18	19	20	21	22	23
24	25	26	27	28	29	30
31						

JUNE

Mo	Tu	We	Th	Fr	Sa	Su
	1	2	3	4	5	6
7	8	9	10	11	12	13
14	15	16	17	18	19	20
21	22	23	24	25	26	27
28	29	30				

JUJY

Mo	Tu	We	Th	Fr	Sa	Su
			1	2	3	4
5	6	7	8	9	10	11
12	13	14	15	16	17	18
19	20	21	22	23	24	25
26	27	28	29	30	31	

AUGUST

Mo	Tu	We	Th	Fr	Sa	Su
						1
2	3	4	5	6	7	8
9	10	11	12	13	14	15
16	17	18	19	20	21	22
23	24	25	26	27	28	29
30	31					

SEPTEMBER

Mo	Tu	We	Th	Fr	Sa	Su
		1	2	3	4	5
6	7	8	9	10	11	12
13	14	15	16	17	18	19
20	21	22	23	24	25	26
27	28	29	30			

OCTOBER

Mo	Tu	We	Th	Fr	Sa	Su
				1	2	3
4	5	6	7	8	9	10
11	12	13	14	15	16	17
18	19	20	21	22	23	24
25	26	27	28	29	30	31

NOVEMBER

Mo	Tu	We	Th	Fr	Sa	Su
1	2	3	4	5	6	7
8	9	10	11	12	13	14
15	16	17	18	19	20	21
22	23	24	25	26	27	28
29	30					

DECEMBER

Mo	Tu	We	Th	Fr	Sa	Su
		1	2	3	4	5
6	7	8	9	10	11	12
13	14	15	16	17	18	19
20	21	22	23	24	25	26
27	28	29	30	31		

a. Which months have 5 Sundays?

____

b. Which day falls on 2nd April?

____

c. Name the month that comes in between April and June.

____

d. Independence Day comes on 15th August every year. Which day will fall on this day in 2021?

____

SKILL UP!

Project

Make a time table of your daily routine after coming home from school.

Lunch	Playing	Studying	Dinner	Sleeping

Life Skills

Rahul has a routine of doing his self-study at 5:30 in the evening.

He has a class test on Thursday.

On Tuesday, he went to play cricket at 5 o'clock and returned home at 7:30. He could not spend time on self-study on Tuesday.

On Wednesday, he again went to play. He returned home at 7 o'clock. He again could not spend time on self-study.

On Thursday, he did not perform well in the class test.

Do you know why?

How should he set his time table to study as well as play cricket?

Do you think we should practise the class lessons at home?

Do you think time is precious?

Mind Buzzer

1. Kriti decided to eat two apples every day. She had ten apples. If she starts eating apples from Tuesday, which day will she be able to finish the apples?
2. When do you think is the next leap year?

Teacher's Notes

- Students can be given dummy clocks to understand 'TIME'.
- Students can relate the days of the week to their time table in school.
- Using the knuckles and the grooves in the hands helps to understand the number of days in a month.
- The students can relate to the seasons with the weather in their own town.

WORKSHEET

Name the seasons. What special features do you see in these seasons? Sequence the seasons from 1 to 5 in the space provided. One has been done for you.

1. 

Name:

Feature:

[ ]

2. 

Name:

Feature:

[ ]

3. 

Name:

Feature:

[1]

4. 

Name:

Feature:

[ ]

5. 

Name:

Feature:

[ ]

13 Data Handling

Learning Objectives

- To learn how to organize data and make lists
- To learn how to compare data and find results

Let's Get Started

It was Nick's birthday. Here are some balloons, a cake, some doughnuts and sweets. Some children are happy having ice creams in the birthday celebration.

1. There are _____ balloons in all.
2. There are _____ candles on the cake.
3. The number of doughnuts is _____.
4. The number of children eating ice creams is _____.
5. The number of red balloons is _____.
6. _____ girls are wearing hats.
7. Yellow balloons are more than green balloons. True or False? _____
8. The number of candles on the cake is _____. Nick is _____ years old now.

MAKING LISTS

When we observe objects, we can count them, observe their colours, their arrangements or positions, etc. It helps us to answer the questions about those objects.

1. Given below are the number of different coloured flowers growing in Arpana's garden.

List of Flowers:

a. The number of red flowers = 5
b. The number of yellow flowers = 4
c. The number of pink flowers = 4
d. The number of purple flowers = 3
e. The number of orange flowers = 2

> **Note**
> Making lists helps to organize data and work on it in an easier way.

Answer the following.

a. What is the total number of flowers in Arpana's garden? **5 + 4 + 4 + 3 + 2 = 18**
b. Which colour flowers are the most in the garden? **Red**.
c. Which colour flowers are the least in the garden? **Orange**.
d. How many more red flowers are there than purple flowers? **2**.
e. Which colour flowers are equal in number? **Yellow and Pink**.

2. The following chart shows the number of chocolate boxes a shopkeeper sold during the week. Observe the chart and answer the questions.

a. What is the total number of chocolate boxes the shopkeeper sold during the week? **1 + 2 + 3 + 2 + 4 + 5 + 6 = 23**
b. How many boxes of chocolates did he sell on Friday? 4
c. On which day did he sell just one box of chocolate? **Monday**
d. On which day did he sell the most number of boxes? **Sunday**

Fill in the blanks.

a. He sold __________ boxes on Wednesday.

b. He sold __________ boxes each on Tuesday and Thursday.

c. He sold __________ more boxes on Saturday than Friday.

EXERCISE 13A

1. In one day, a shopkeeper sold the following items. Observe the items and answer the questions.

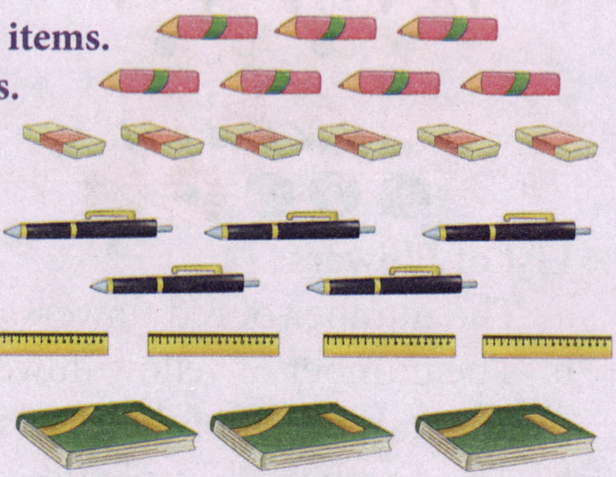

a. List the items sold by the shopkeeper.

Pencils __________

Erasers __________

Pens __________

Rulers __________

Notebooks __________

b. What is the total number of items sold by him? __________

c. How many more pencils did he sell than notebooks? __________

d. Which item did he sell the most in number? __________

e. Which item did he sell the least in number? __________

f. How many more erasers did he sell than notebooks? __________

2. Johny and his mother were playing with colourful blocks. They created different shapes using the blocks. Answer the following.

a. List the number of blocks.

Red _____ Yellow _____ Blue _____ Green _____

b. What is the total number of blocks? _____

c. How many types of colours are used? _____

d. The number of cubes is _____.

e. The total number of cubes and cuboids is _____.

f. The number of yellow-coloured blocks is _____ (less/greater) than the number of blue-coloured blocks.

Mental Maths

1. **Consider the pattern.**

   2, 2, 2, 3, 3, 3, 4, 4, 4, 5, 5, 5

   a. How many numbers are there? ________

   b. How many times is a number repeated? ________

2. **Neha has 11 chocolates, Sneha has 8 chocolates and Meera has 16 chocolates.**

   a. If they start eating the chocolates, who will be able to finish eating earlier? ________

   b. Who has the maximum number of chocolates? ________

   c. Find the difference between the number of chocolates with Neha and Sneha. ________

Go Easy!

- Data handling can become much easier if you observe data in your surroundings, say items in your school bag, in your kitchen, in your classroom, etc. and then make comparisons and find results.
- The most important thing is to make a list of all the items first.

PUZZLE!

Observe the picture. Make a list of the following.

1. Number of trees ____
2. Number of marbles on the ground ____
3. Number of children ____
4. Number of boys ____
5. Number of girls ____
6. Number of balls ____

If there are five more marbles in the red bag carried by one of the boys in the picture, what will be the total number of marbles then?

Maths Lab Activity

Aim: To reinforce the method of organizing and comparing data and finding results

Materials required: A pen, notebook

Procedure: 1. Write down the following two words in your notebooks.

Alphabetical and Education

2. Read and write the vowels in these two words.
   But before proceeding, write down all the vowels of the English alphabets. ________

Words	Number of vowels
Alphabetical	5
Education	5

3. We notice that there are same number of vowels in both the words.
   Vowels in 'Alphabetical': a, a, e, i, a
   Vowels in 'Education': e, u, a, i, o
4. What do we observe?
   Which word contains all the vowels? ____________
   Which vowels are missing in the word, Alphabetical? ____________
5. Find out more such words which contain all the vowels of the English alphabet.
   ____________, ____________, ____________, ____________

Concept Map

Data Handling

- Collecting data
- Organizing data
- Understanding data
- Finding results

Key Concepts

- **Data** is the information collected.
- **Organizing** data means placing the data in a way so that we can understand it.
- After organizing data, we can prepare lists and **understand** data easily.
- Final step is to find the **results**.

Chapter Revision

A. Meena went to the market and bought the following items . Observe the items and answer the questions.

1. How many dresses did Meena buy? ____________
2. How many pens did Meena buy? ____________
3. How many more pens did Meena buy than belts? ____________
4. How many more books did Meena buy than dresses? ____________
5. How many pairs of shoes did Meena buy? ____________

B. An ice cream vendor sold the following number of ice creams during the week. Observe the chart and answer the questions.

1. List the number of ice creams sold on each day.
2. What is the total number of ice creams sold by him in the week? ____________
3. How many more ice creams did he sell on Friday than Monday? ____________
4. On which day did he sell the least number of ice creams? ____________
5. On which day did he sell the maximum number of ice creams? ____________
6. On which two days did he sell the same number of ice creams? ____________

SKILL UP!

Project

Collect some stamps from Monday to Friday.

- List down how many stamps you collected each day.
- Find out the day on which you collected the least and the maximum number of stamps.
- How many stamps did you collect on Thursday and Monday?
- Was the number of stamps collected on Friday more than the number of stamps collected on Tuesday?

Life Skills

Given here is a list of students and their hobbies.

Hobbies	Names of Students
Dancing	Tina, Megha, Anu
Swimming	Renu, John, Bill, Annie, Sara
Singing	Akshay

1. Count and write the number of students who like

   Dancing ______, Swimming _______ and Singing ______

2. The teacher wants to arrange the class into two groups for dancing and swimming competitions. Who will not be able to take part in the competitions? Do you think he should be given a chance to show his talent?

Mind Buzzer

Tanya read 7 storybooks, Manya read 5 storybooks and Kavya read 8 storybooks in 20 days. Who has the best speed in reading a storybook?

Kavya read one storybook more than Tanya. Do you think Tanya has the capability to gain speed in reading? Can Tanya and Kavya be equally good in reading speed?

Teacher's Notes

1. Explain students how a data is organized by giving real-life examples.
2. After organizing data, they will be able to recall and strengthen their concepts on counting, comparing, arranging and managing data.
3. Ask them to practise more questions and derive results that can help them to enhance their prior knowledge as well.

WORKSHEET

Following is the list of students who like to watch different channels on TV.

Channel	Number of Students
Cartoon Channel	15
News Channel	2
Sports Channel	9

Cartoon Channel

News Channel

Sports Channel

Observe the list above and answer the questions.

a. Which channel is liked by the most number of students? __________

b. Which channel is liked by the least number of students? __________

c. How many students like to watch the sports channel? __________

d. How many more students like to watch the cartoon channel than the news channel?

____

e. Write the total number of students according to the given data above. __________

f. Three more students join the list of students liking the sports channel. How many students like the sports channel now? __________

REASONING WORKSHEET 3

1. **Vidya wants to buy a doll for ₹450. She collects ₹100 every day for 5 days. Tick (✓) the correct options.**

   a. She can buy the doll for ₹590.
   b. She cannot buy the doll for ₹500.
   c. She can buy the doll for ₹500.
   d. She cannot buy the doll for ₹505.

2. **Wanshan had ₹500 and Anmol had ₹300. They wanted to share a pizza which costs ₹500. Tick (✓) the correct options.**

   a. They can together buy the pizza.
   b. Wanshan alone can buy the pizza.
   c. Anmol alone can buy the pizza.
   d. They cannot buy the pizza.

3. **When should Suklin take out woollen clothes to wear?**

   a. March b. September c. June d. December

4. **Jinnie goes to park to play for 2 hours. She goes at 5 o'clock. When should she return home?**

   a. 8 o'clock b. 7 o'clock c. 6 o'clock d. 5 o'clock

5. **Greg read the following number of pages from a storybook in 4 days.**

   Monday - 5 pages, Tuesday - 3 pages, Wednesday - 6 pages, Thursday - 2 pages

   a. He read 18 pages in 4 days.
   b. He got more time to read on Wednesday.
   c. He got less time to read on Tuesday.
   d. He read 1 page more on Tuesday than on Thursday.

REVIEW CORNER

Review 1 **Chapters 1-3**

Maximum Marks = 40

A. Choose the correct option. **[1 × 3]**

1. The place value of 7 in 479 is

   a. 40 b. 70 c. 90 d. 700

2. 1 added to the greatest 2-digit number is

   a. 98 b. 99 c. 100 d. 101

3. The tens digit in the result of 78 – 25 is

   a. 7 b. 2 c. 6 d. 5

B. Fill in the blanks. **[2 × 3]**

1. Arrange the numbers in descending order.

   59, 49, 51, 54,55

   ____

2. a. The two numbers that come in between 87 and 91 are

   ______________________________.

   b. Number name for the smallest 3-digit number is

   ______________________________.

3. 25 subtracted from the greatest 2-digit number is

   ______________________________.

Rough Work

C. Solve the following. [3 × 5]

1. a. Write >, < or =.

   98 ☐ 89

   b. The sum of 45 and 1 gives ________. The result is the _________ (successor/predecessor) of 45.

	T	O
+		

   c. One hundred forty-nine is written as _______.

2. Subtract 45 from 87.
   Is the result an odd number?

   ____

	T	O
−		

3. Solve 24 + 53 vertically.
   Write the predecessor of the result.

   ____

	T	O
+		

4. 3 tens + 5 tens = _______. Subtract the result from 9 tens.
   Show vertical subtraction.

5. Solve 67 + 24 + 13.

	T	O
+		

Rough Work

D. Answer the following questions. [4 × 4]

1. Add the successor of 85 to 18.
   Write the number name of the result.

   ____

T	O
+	

2. Sukher skipped 23 times on Monday and 51 times on Tuesday. How many times did Sukher skip on both the days?

T	O
+	

3. Find the difference between 76 and 37.
   Write the place value of all the digits in the result.

T	O
–	

4. Out of 294 books, the teacher distributed 38 books. How many books were left?

T	O
–	

Rough Work

Review 2 | **Chapters 4-7**

Maximum Marks = 40

A. Write T for True and F for False. **[1 × 3]**

1. The numeral for seven hundred nine is 790. ☐
2. The successor of 99 gives the smallest 2-digit number. ☐
3. 5 + 5 + 5 = 3 × 5 ☐

B. Answer the following questions. **[2 × 3]**

1. a. Fill in the blanks using <, > or =.

   349 ☐ 562

   b. 611 – 111 = ________

H	T	O
–		

2. Write the smallest and the greatest number using the digits 0, 3 and 8.

Digits	Smallest number	Greatest number
0		
3		
8		

3. Solve 54 × 3.

T	O
×	

Rough Work

C. Solve the following. **[3 × 5]**

1. a. Write the smallest 4-digit number and write its number name.
   b. Write the place value and face value of the digits in 524.
   c. Complete the pattern: 235, 335, ____, ____, ____, ____

2. a. Write the short form of 600 + 20 + 6. Write its number name.
   b. Fill in the missing numbers on the number line.

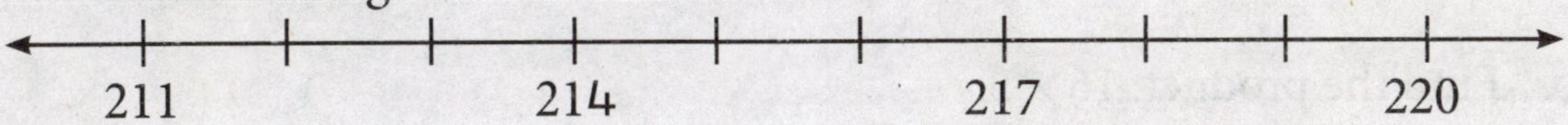

   c. Find the sum: 122 + 33 + 2.

H	T	O
+		

3. Solve 233 + 254 + 312.
   Write the number name of the result.
   ____

T	O
+	

4. Solve 87 – 28.
   Find the predecessor of the result.
   ____

T	O
–	

5. a. Write the multiplication statements for the following repeated additions.
   5 + 5 + 5 + 5 = _____ and 7 + 7 + 7 + 7 + 7 = _____
   b. Express 4 × 2 on the number line. Find the product.

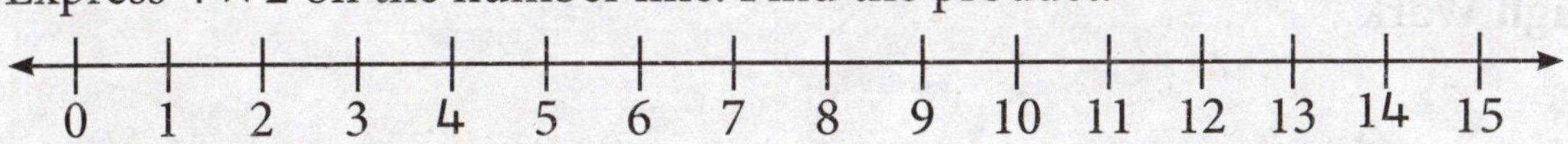

   c. Find the product of 24 and 8.

T	O
×	

Rough Work

D. Answer the following questions. [4 × 4]

1. a. What is the difference between 984 and 152?

H	T	O
−		

   b. Find the product: 16 × 5.

T	O
×	

2. There are 253 boys and 257 girls in a school. How many children are there in the school?

H	T	O
+		

3. Out of 796 cars in a parking area, 243 cars were white in colour. How many cars were not white?

H	T	O
−		

4. A packet contains 4 doughnuts. How many doughnuts are there in 6 packets?

T	O
×	

Rough Work

Review 3 **Chapters 8-10**

Maximum Marks = 40

A. Match the following. [1 × 3]

1. 5 ÷ 1 — 10 cm
2. Length of a pen — square
3.  — 5

B. Fill in the blanks. [2 × 3]

1. a. 2 ÷ 2 = ______. b. 99 ÷ 0 = ______.
2. a. The mass of potatoes will be measured in ______.
   b. A teaspoon measures about ______ mℓ of a liquid.
3. a. An oval has ______ straight edges and ______ corners.
   b. Complete the pattern: X, X, Z, X, X, ______, ______, ______, ______

C. Solve and answer. [3 × 5]

1. Solve 8 ÷ 2 using repeated subtraction.
2. Put 6 flowers equally in 3 vases. How many flowers are there in each vase?
   Write the division statement. ________________
3. a. 1 m = ____ cm b. 1 kg = ____ g c. 1 ℓ = ______ mℓ
4. Tick (✓) the correct answer.

Rectangle/Circle

Triangle/Rectangle

Rectangle/Square

5. Complete the patterns.
   a. 2, 4, 6, 8, ______, ______ b. L, M, N, O, L, M, _____, _____, _____
   c.  ______, ______, ______

Rough Work

D. Solve and answer. [4 × 4]

1. Solve 10 ÷ 2 using the number line.

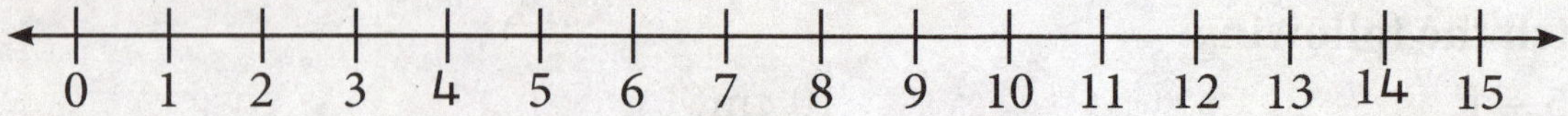

2. Sam wants to eat 12 toffees in 6 days. How many toffees should he eat every day?

Sam should eat _____ toffees every day.

3. a. 56 ÷ 8 = _____

   b. The length of a bed can be 3 metres. True/False

   c. Complete the pattern.

___________, ___________

   d. Write V for vertical line, H for horizontal line and S for slanting line.

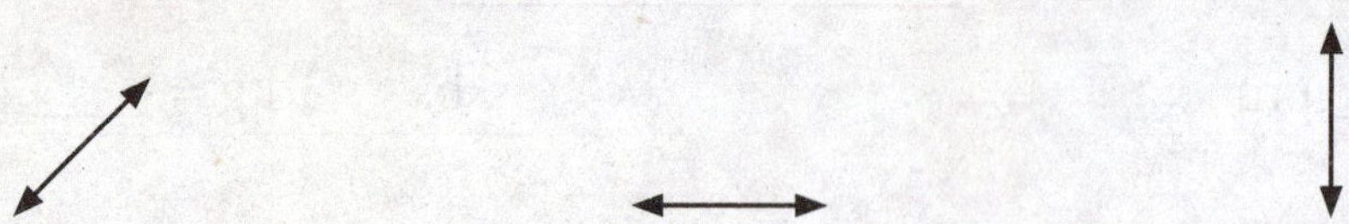

_______________ _______________ _______________

4. Write R for rolling object, S for sliding object and RS for rolling and sliding object.

__________ __________ __________ __________.

Rough Work

Review 4 **Chapters 11–13**

Maximum Marks = 40

A. Match the following. **[1 × 3]**

1.  The first day of the week
2.  10
3. Monday 5 o'clock

B. Fill in the blanks. **[2 × 3]**

1. a.  +  = ₹ ____________

   b.  +  +  = ₹ ____________

2. a. If Today is Friday, then tomorrow will be ____________.

   b. ______ season comes after the winter season.

3. Aayushi bought the given items. Answer the following questions.

   a. She bought ________ notebooks and ________ pens.

   b. The total number of items is ________.

C. Solve and answer. **[3 × 5]**

1. Fill in the blanks using >, < or =.

   a.  ☐  + 

   b.  ☐  + 

   c.  +  ☐  + 

Rough Work

2. A fruit basket costs ₹485. Give two combinations of notes and coins that can be given by her to the fruit seller.

3. Look at the clock given below and answer the questions.

   a. I went to my friend's house at __________.

   b. July has __________ days.

   c. Snowfall is seen at some places during the __________ season.

4. Meg and Jon drank 6 glasses of juice on Monday, 5 glasses on Tuesday and 6 glasses on Wednesday.

   a. On which two days did they drink the same amount of juice? __________

   b. The sum of the number of juice glasses on Monday and Tuesday is __________.

   c. How many glasses of juice did they drink on all the three days? __________

5. Consider the pattern.

   3, 3, 3, 4, 4, 4, 4, 5, 5, 5, 5, 5, 5, 6, 6

   a. How many times each number is repeated? __________

   b. How many numbers are there? __________

   c. 6 occurs twice and 3 occurs thrice. True or False? __________

Rough Work

D. Answer the following questions. [4 × 4]

1. A toy bus costs ₹380 and a toy aeroplane cost ₹590. Which toy costs more and by how much?
2. a. I purchased a dress for ₹870. I gave the shopkeeper ₹990.
   How much money will I get in return from the shopkeeper?
   b. What kind of clothes do we need in summer season? (Woollen, Cotton, Raincoats)
3. a. I reached the market at 5:00 in the evening. I left the market after one hour. Draw the hands of the clock to show the time when she left the market.

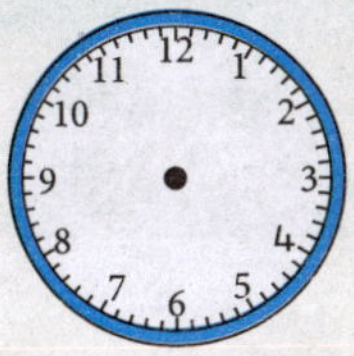

   b. Write the names of the third, seventh and tenth months of the year.
4. An ice cream vender sold the following ice creams one day.

Vanilla	5
Chocolate	8
Mango	7
Strawberry	9

   a. Which ice cream did he sell the most in number?
   b. Which flavours of ice creams did he sell more than Mango?
   c. Which ice cream is bought the least in number?
   d. What is the total numbers of ice creams that he sold?

Rough Work

CLASS 2

QUESTION PAPER SET A

IMO

SOF INTERNATIONAL MATHEMATICS OLYMPIAD 2018-19

DO NOT OPEN THIS BOOKLET UNTIL ASKED TO DO SO

Total Questions: 35 | Time: 1 hr.

Guidelines for the Candidate

1. Please check your Name, Class and Section on the OMR sheet provided to you. In case, OMR sheet with your name is missing, please fill in information about yourself in the blank OMR sheet provided before start of exam.
2. Please fill in your **Mobile Number** clearly on the OMR Sheet and do not forget to sign it. We will share with you your marks / result on your mobile number.
3. The Question Paper comprises four sections:

   Logical Reasoning (10 Questions), **Mathematical Reasoning** (10 Questions), **Everyday Mathematics** (10 Questions) and **Achievers Section** (5 Questions)

   Each question in Achievers Section carries 2 marks, whereas all other questions carry one mark each.
4. All questions are compulsory. There is no negative marking. Use of calculator is not permitted.
5. There is only ONE correct answer. Choose only ONE option for an answer.
6. To mark your choice of answers by darkening the circles on the OMR Sheet, use **HB Pencil** or **Blue / Black ball point pen** only. E.g.

   Q.16: Sonia had 80 sweets. She gave 15 sweets to Danish and 15 sweets to Megha. How many sweets are left with her?

   A. 50 B. 30 C. 60 D. 40

   As the correct answer is option A, you must darken the circle corresponding to option A on the OMR Sheet. 16. ● Ⓑ Ⓒ Ⓓ
7. Rough work should be done in the blank space provided in the booklet.
8. Return the OMR Sheet to the invigilator at the end of the exam.
9. Please fill in your personal details in the space provided on this page before attempting the paper.

SOF
SCIENCE OLYMPIAD FOUNDATION
Inspiring Young Minds Through Knowledge Olympiads

Name:..

Section:............. SOF Olympiad Roll No.:........................ Contact No.:...

1. Find the missing number, if the same rule is followed in all the three figures.

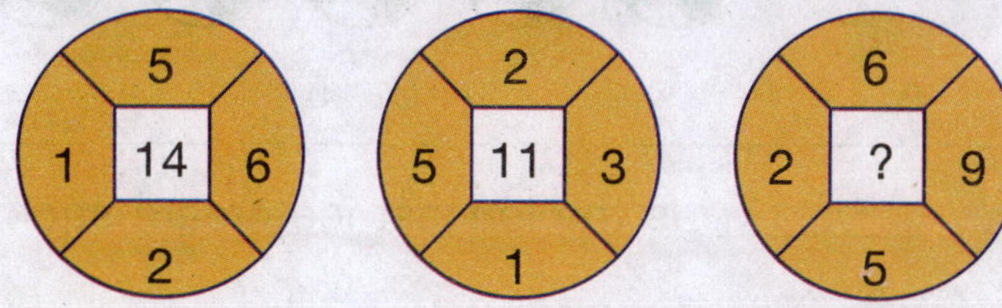

A. 24
B. 22
C. 23
D. 20

---

2. Find the odd one out.

A.  B.  C.  D. 

---

3. If every Sunday is a holiday and Tarun was on leave on all Mondays and all Wednesdays of April 20XX, then the total number of days Tarun didn't go to office is ________.

A. 10
B. 14
C. 12
D. 13

APRIL 20XX

S	M	T	W	Th	F	S
	1	2	3	4	5	6
7	8	9	10	11	12	13
14	15	16	17	18	19	20
21	22	23	24	25	26	27
28	29	30				

---

4. Pencil ________ is second to the left of third pencil from the right end.

A. N
B. K
C. O
D. L

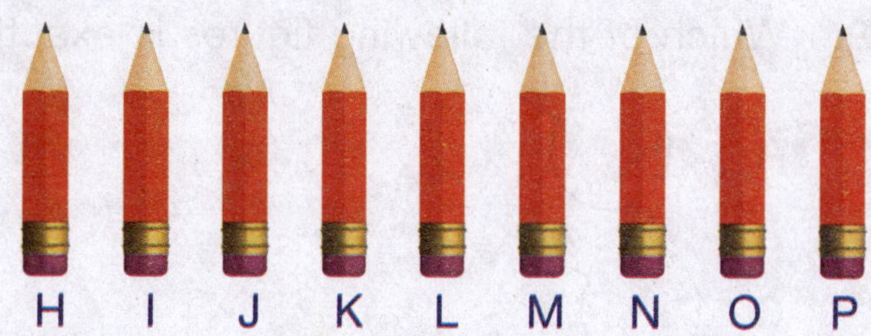

---

5. If  is called ,  is called  and  is called , then what will you blow out at the time of your birthday celebration?

A.  B.  C.  D. 

SPACE FOR ROUGH WORK

6. How many groups of 2 footballs each can be formed from the given footballs?

A. 4 B. 5 C. 2 D. 6

7. ________ is the longest ice cream stick and ________ is the shortest ice cream stick.

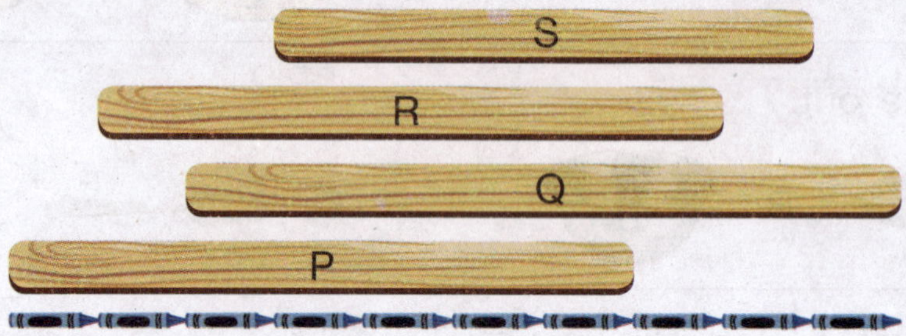

A. Q, R B. Q, S C. P, R D. P, Q

8. There are __________ rectangles and ______ circles in the given figure.

A. 4, 20

B. 3, 22

C. 4, 21

D. 3, 21

9. Which of the following figures is exactly embedded in the given figure as one of its parts?

A. 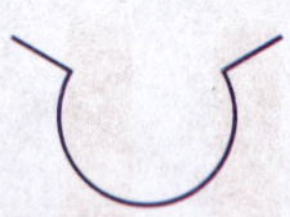

B. 

C. 

D. 

10. If 'Diwali' is related to  in some way, then in the same way 'Holi' is related to ________.

A. 

B. 

C. 

D. 

SPACE FOR ROUGH WORK

11. What is the height of the tree (in m) shown here?

A. 35
B. 32
C. 33
D. 34

---

12. 317 more than 218 is ________.

A. Five hundred sixteen
B. Five hundred twenty six
C. Five hundred forty five
D. Five hundred thirty five

---

13. Which of the following shapes have no curved lines?

A. R and S
B. T, P and R
C. R and T
D. R, T and U

---

14. Which of the following options correctly shows increasing order of the given set of numbers?

A. 508, 516, 531, 599
B. 508, 516, 599, 531
C. 531, 516, 599, 508
D. 508, 599, 516, 531

---

15. Select the subtraction sentence that shows the given condition.
"Number of balls with even numbers subtracted from the total number of balls is equal to the number of balls with odd numbers".

A. 18 – 5 = 13
B. 18 – 6 = 12
C. 18 – 10 = 8
D. 18 – 18 = 0

---

16. I am an odd number. I am more than (202 + 7) but less than (222 – 9). Who am I?

A. 211
B. 210
C. 209
D. 213

SPACE FOR ROUGH WORK

17. Identify the number.

- The digit at hundred's place is same as that at one's place.
- The digit at ten's place is the largest one digit number.
- The place value of hundred's place digit is 32 tens more than 480.

A. 899 B. 989 C. 988 D. 898

---

18. If  +  +  +  = 50,  +  = 40 and  = 20, then  = _____.

A. 10 B. 20 C. 30 D. 40

Direction (19-20) : The given pictograph shows the number of books sold by a leading book store in 4 different months. Study the graph and answer the following questions.

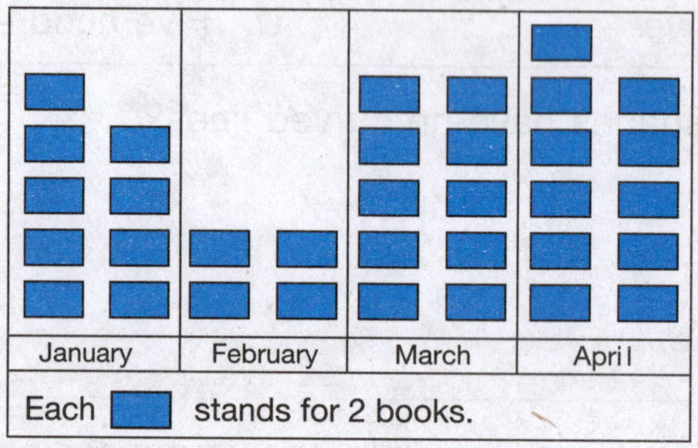

19. How many books were sold in four months altogether ?

A. 94 B. 72 C. 34 D. 68

20. How many more books were sold in January than in February ?

A. 8 B. 5 C. 20 D. 10

EVERYDAY MATHEMATICS

21. Mrs Rai saved ₹ 258 to buy a calculator. How much more amount does she need to buy the given calculator?

A. ₹ 516
B. ₹ 541
C. ₹ 283
D. ₹ 238

---

22. Ramya sold 2 dozen bananas out of 30 bananas and Riya sold 3 dozen bananas out of 40 bananas. Number of bananas left with them altogether is ______.

A. 36 B. 24 C. 70 D. 10

SPACE FOR ROUGH WORK

23. Ankur has the given quantity of paint. If Anish has 21 L of paint more than Ankur, then total quantity of paint they have altogether is __________.

A. 139 L

B. 193 L

C. 59 L

D. 89 L

24. A bus covers 77 km and a car covers 54 km with the same quantity of fuel. Which covers less distance and by how much?

A. Car, 23 km B. Bus, 23 km C. Car, 33 km D. Bus, 33 km

25. Priyanka is trying to make a cube using straws and balls of clay. She uses straws for making edges and clay balls for making corners. How many straws and balls of clay will she need?

A. 6 straws, 8 balls of clay B. 12 straws, 6 balls of clay

C. 8 straws, 6 balls of clay D. 12 straws, 8 balls of clay

26. The starting time and ending time of Ramesh's office is shown here. The duration for which he works in the office is __________.

A. 6 hours 12 mins

B. 9 hours 30 mins

C. 8 hours 30 mins

D. 18 hours 20 mins

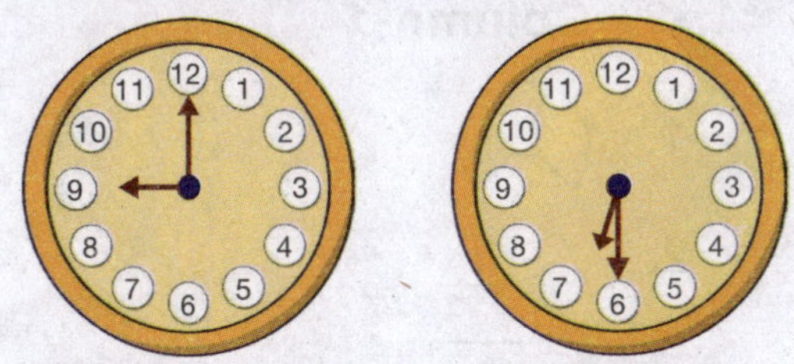

Starting time Ending time

27. Sia has  and . If she gives 2 kites and 2 balloons to each of her 3 friends, then _______ will be left with her.

A. Only 3 kites B. Only 2 balloons

C. 4 kites and 1 balloon D. 2 kites and 1 balloon

28. Rupa bought a pumpkin and a pineapple as shown. What is the total weight of 3 such pumpkins and 2 such pineapples?

A. 21 kg

B. 27 kg

C. 31 kg

D. 30 kg

SPACE FOR ROUGH WORK

29. A shopkeeper sells given trays of eggs in one day. If he sells same number of eggs everyday, then he will sell 72 eggs in ________ days.

A. 6 B. 5 C. 3 D. 4

30. The given table shows the price of 2 types of books in 4 different bookstores.
Bookstore ______ will sale a story book and a drawing book together for maximum amount.

Bookstore	Story Book (in ₹)	Drawing Book (in ₹)
P	400	295
Q	249	750
R	421	320
S	621	341

A. S B. Q
C. R D. P

ACHIEVERS SECTION

31. Match the figures given in Column-1 with their corresponding missing parts given in Column-2 and select the CORRECT option.

Column-1	Column-2
1. 	(a) 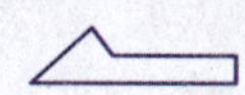
2. 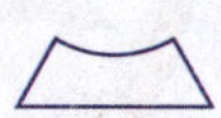	(b) 
3. 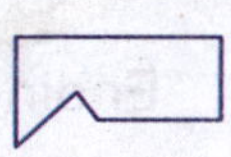	(c) 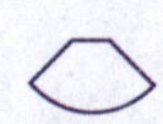
4. 	(d) 

A. 1-(a), 2-(b), 3-(d), 4-(c) B. 1-(a), 2-(c), 3-(b), 4-(d)
C. 1-(c), 2-(d), 3-(a), 4-(b) D. 1-(b), 2-(a), 3-(d), 4-(c)

32. Aman has to travel from his house to the market. Which of the following will be the shortest route?

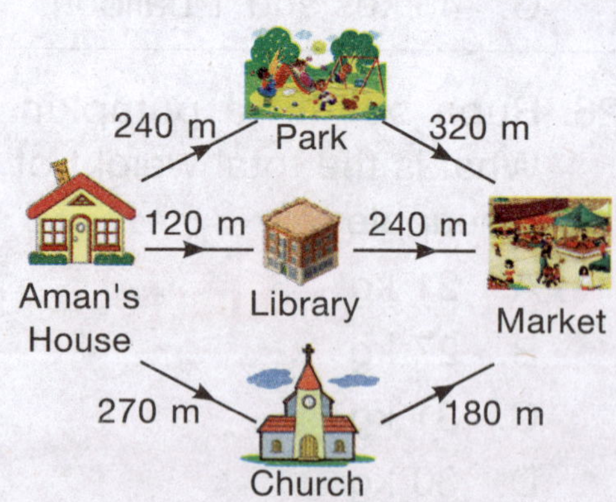

A. House → Park → Market
B. House → Church → Market
C. House → Library → Market
D. All routes have equal distances.

SPACE FOR ROUGH WORK

33. Sum of numbers on which two owls is greater than 650 but less than 700?

A. P and Q
B. Q and R
C. P and R
D. Can't be determined

---

34. Study the timings of daily activities of Payal as shown in the table and fill in the blanks.

- Activities that last for 1 hour in total are ___P___ and ___Q___.
- The activity that lasted for 15 minutes only is ___R___.

Time	Activities
1:30 p.m. – 2:00 p.m.	Reading Book
2:00 p.m. – 2:15 p.m.	Painting
2:15 p.m. – 3:00 p.m.	Doing Homework
3:00 p.m. – 3:30 p.m.	Dance Practice
4:00 p.m. – 4:30 p.m.	Playing Football

	P	Q	R
A.	Reading Book	Playing Football	Reading Book
B.	Playing Football	Reading Book	Dance Practice
C.	Playing Football	Reading Book	Painting
D.	Doing Homework	Playing Football	Reading Book

---

35. Kunal went for shopping and bought one hand bag, two trousers and one cap. He gave one ₹ 100 note and two ₹ 200 notes to the shopkeeper. How much amount of money will he receive back?

A. ₹45 B. ₹25 C. ₹ 55 D. ₹ 35

ANSWER KEYS

1.	(B)	**2.**	(D)	**3.**	(D)	**4.**	(D)	**5.**	(C)	**6.**	(B)	**7.**	(B)
8.	(C)	**9.**	(A)	**10.**	(B)	**11.**	(D)	**12.**	(D)	**13.**	(C)	**14.**	(A)
15.	(C)	**16.**	(A)	**17.**	(D)	**18.**	(A)	**19.**	(D)	**20.**	(D)	**21.**	(B)
22.	(D)	**23.**	(A)	**24.**	(A)	**25.**	(D)	**26.**	(B)	**27.**	(D)	**28.**	(C)
29.	(C)	**30.**	(B)	**31.**	(C)	**32.**	(C)	**33.**	(B)	**34.**	(C)	**35.**	(D)

SOF SCIENCE OLYMPIAD FOUNDATION

National Office: Plot 99, First Floor, Sector 44 Institutional area, Gurgaon -122 003 (HR) India
Email: info@sofworld.org | Website: www.sofworld.org
Regd. Office: 406, Taj Apt., Ring Road, New Delhi-110 029
Note: Please address all communication to the National Office only.

ANSWERS

Chapter 1

Exercise 1A

1 a. 108 – One hundred eight
b. 161 – One hundred sixty-one

2. a. 170 b. 187

3. a. One hundred forty-three
b. One hundred fifty-five

4. a. 135 – One hundred thirty-five
b. 103 – One hundred three
c. 100 - One hundred
d. 148 – One hundred forty-eight
e. 176 – One hundred seventy-six

5.

151	152	153	154	155	156	157	158	159	160
161	**162**	163	164	165	166	167	168	**169**	170
171	172	173	174	**175**	**176**	177	178	179	180
181	182	183	184	185	186	187	188	189	**190**
191	192	193	**194**	195	196	**197**	198	199	**200**

6. a. 162 b. 197

7. a. 199 b. 126

8. 189, 188, 187, 186

9. 166 10. 111

Exercise 1B

1. a. Face Value – 7 Place Value - 7
b. Face Value – 8 Place Value - 80

2. a. 100 + 50 + 0 b. 100 + 0 + 0
c. 100 + 40 + 1 d. 100 + 10 + 3

3. a. 109 b. 167 c. 105 d. 123

4. a. 100 + 30 + 2 b. 100 + 10 + 5

Exercise 1C

1. a. 135 b. 200 c. 111 d. 165

2. a. 111 b. 109 c. 122 d. 116

3. a. 175 < 185 b. 146 > 144
c. 198 < 200 d. 153 = 153

4. a. 194 b. 108 c. 147 d. 195

Exercise 1D

1. a. 10, 110, 130, 155, 166, 190
b. 45, 107, 111, 151, 170, 189

2. a. 200, 199, 198, 195, 192, 191
b. 188, 181, 118, 110, 108, 106

Exercise 1E

1. a. first b. third c. fifth d. fourth
e. false f. second

2. a. B b. seventh c. J, I d. E, purple
e. false f. second

Exercise 1F

1. House A - 150, 142, 4, 160, 194
House B - 125, 21, 161

2. b. 10, even c. 4, even
d. 9, odd e. 3, odd
f. 8, even

3. 

Chapter Revision

A. 1. 172; One hundred seventy-two
2. 50 3. 1

B. 171, 172, 173, 174, 175, 176, 177, 178

C. 1. 109, 166, 175, 181, 190; 190, 181, 175, 166, 109
2. 101, 110, 111, 114, 117; 117, 114, 111, 110, 101

D. 1. Ball 2. Tennis racket and ball
3. sixth 4. fifth 5. fourth

E. Bag A – 200, 136, 140, 18, 192, 100, 62, 178
Bag B – 49, 5, 165

Worksheet

1. Box A – Hat, Bow
Box B – Earrings, Balloon
Box C – Banana, Cookie
Box D – T-shirt, Rose
Box E – Pen, Butterfly

2. Across: 1. 103 2. 124 5. 169 7. 198
Down: 1. 112 2. 135 3. 146 4. 150 6. 172

Chapter 2

Exercise 2A

1. a. 8 b. 55 c. 83 d. 137

2. a. 5 b. 7 + 3 = 10 c. 3 + 4 = 7

Exercise 2B

1. a. 11 b. 94 c. 11 d. 82
2. a. 73 b. 90 c. 45 d. 84

Exercise 2C

1. a. 8 b. 9 c. 17 d. 16
2. a. 69 b. 97 c. 68 d. 96

Exercise 2D

a. 82 b. 40 c. 103 d. 95

Exercise 2E

1. 66 books 2. 93 samosas and pizzas
3. 84 pages 4. 85 pens 5. 68 bottles

Chapter Revision

A. 1. b. 2. b. 3. c.
B. 1. 50 + 30 = 8 tens
2. 20 + 21 + 35 = 35 + 21 + 20
3. 7 + 8 + 2 = 17
4. Ninety-five = 48 + 10 + 37
5. 1 + 29 = Thirty
C. 1. 64 2. 18 3. 84 4. 66
D. 1. 70 2. 110 3. 60 4. 1
E. 1. T 2. F 3. F
F. 1. 10 + 99 = 109 2. 94 marks

Worksheet

Anu: green balloon – 1, yellow balloon – 6
Hazel: blue balloon – 30, yellow balloon - 12

Chapter 3

Exercise 3A

1. 78 2. 35 3. 68 4. 34
5. 56 6. 18 7. 35 8. 35

Exercise 3B

1. 161 2. 125 3. 52 4. 121

Exercise 3C

1. 131 2. 82 3. 55 4. 142

Exercise 3D

1. 121 2. 101
3. 22 toffees 4. 45 red cars
5. 111 pink roses 6. 115 chairs

Chapter Revision

A. 1. 136 2. 141 3. 150 4. 114
B. 45, Circle the numbers – 174, 89, 62, 158, 180
C. 1. 54 2.113 3. 36 4. 142
D. 1. 131 2. 82
E. 1. F 2. F 3. F 4. T
F. 1. 88 2. 72 3. 16
G. 1. a. 148 balloons b. 142 balloons
2. 153 monkeys 3. 124 children

Worksheet

Parts a., c., e., g., i. and k. are equal to 68. Colour these in orange. Parts b., d., f., h., j. and l. are equal to 42. Colour these in yellow. Part m. = 66. Colour this in blue. Parts n., o., p. and q are equal to 56. Colour these in light green.

Chapter 4

Exercise 4A

1. a. 421, Four hundred twenty-one
b. 834, Eight hundred thirty-four
2. a. 9 hundreds 0 tens 6 ones, Nine hundred six
b. 2 hundreds 4 tens 3 ones, Two hundred forty-three
3. a. 431 b. 963 c. 619 d. 871
4. a. 473 b. 862
5. a. 363, 364, 365 b. 575, 576, 577
c. 194, 195, 196 d. 846, 847, 848

Exercise 4B

1. 323, 324, 326, 327, 328
2. 542, 543, 545, 546, 548, 549
3. 832, 833, 834, 836, 837, 839, 840
4. 672, 673, 674, 676, 677, 679

Exercise 4C

1. a. Pace Value: 1= 100 7 = 70 3 = 3
Face Value: 1=1 7 = 7 3 = 3
b. Place Value: 6 = 600 8 = 80 4 = 4
Face Value: 6=6 8 = 8 4 = 4
2. a. 3 hundreds 8 tens 5 ones, 300 + 80 + 5
b. 6 hundreds 9 tens 1 one, 600 + 90 + 1
3. a. 300 b. 70 c. 2
4. a. 4 b. 9 c. 6
5. a. 532 b. 7 c. 40 d. 900 + 9

Exercise 4D

1. a. 964 > 182 b. 729 > 607
c. 200 < 800 d. 521 < 906
e. 374 = 374 f. 189 > 183
2. a 569 b. 843 c. 489
3. a. 478 b. 238 c. 341

Exercise 4E

1. a. 127, 349, 623, 805 b. 158, 673, 691, 908
2. a. 640, 573, 257, 189 b. 928, 746, 329, 150
3. a. 560, 570, 580, 590 b. 576, 676, 776, 876
   c. 760, 750, 740, 730 d. 920, 910, 900, 890

Exercise 4F

1. a. 136 b. 624 c. 468 d. 855
2. a. 274 b. 497 c. 613 d. 800
3. a. 235 b. 722 c. 947 d. 670, 671
4. 446, 447
5. 868, 869, 870

Exercise 4G

1. 83, 38 2. 51, 15 3. 920, 209 4. 764, 467

Chapter Revision

A. 1. 4 hundreds 3 tens 8 ones, Four hundred thirty-eight
   2. 2 hundreds 2 tens 8 ones, Two hundred twenty-eight
   3. 999 4. 653 5. 930
   6. 811, 812, 819, 821, 919

B. 623, 624, 626, 628, 629

C. 1. One hundred twenty-five
   2. 100 + 20 + 5
   3. Place Value = 20, Face Value = 2

D. 1. F 2. F 3. T 4. F 5. F

E. 1. 431 < 485 2. 221 > 212
   3. 398 < 432 4. 817 < 877

F. 1. 710, 810, 910 2. 830, 840, 850, 870, 880

G. 456

H. 238, 239, 240 and 241

I. 985, 986, 987, 988

J. 211, Two hundred eleven

Worksheet

1. a. Six hundred seventy
   b. Six hundred eighty
   c. Seven hundred eighty
   d. Nine hundred twenty
2. 7 – 700, 8 – 80, 0 – 0
3. Bananas 4. Bananas 5. Strawberries
6. Apples
7. Strawberries, Grapes, Bananas, Apples

Chapter 5

Exercise 5A

1. a. 129 b. 120 c. 111 d. 125
2. 121 coins 3. 137 flowers

Exercise 5B

1. 179 2. 154 3. 198 4. 277

Exercise 5C

1. 967 2. 899 3. 973 4. 968

Exercise 5D

1. 272 2. 358 3. 556 4. 127

Exercise 5E

1. 368 people 2. 394 books
3. 479 ice creams 4. 698 marbles

Chapter Revision

A. 1. 83 2. 167

B. 1. 700 2. 10 + 245 = 255
   3. 520 4. 133 5. 610, 710, 810
   6. Three hundred fifty

C. 1. 746 2. 975 3. 47 4. 85
   5. 658 6. 900

D. 1. 100 + 400 = Five hundred
   2. 150 + 20 = One hundred seventy
   3. 220 + 45 = Two hundred sixty-five
   4. 350 + 130 = Four hundred eighty

E. 1. F 2. F 3. F 4. T

F. 1. 372 tables and chairs 2. 699 rose plants
   3. 51 dolls 4. 568 students

Worksheet

a. 564 b. 528 c. 129 d. 318
e. 364 f. 718 g. 501 h. 258
i. 985 j. 557 k. 937

Colour the parts f., i. and k. in red. Colour the parts a., b., g. and j. in pink. Colour the parts c., d., e., and h. in blue.

Chapter 6

Exercise 6A

1. 261 2. 325 3. 352 4. 811

Exercise 6B

1. 511 2. 742 3. 528 4. 265

Exercise 6C

1. 621 2. 501 3. 576 – 304 = 272
4. 774 – 651 = 123

Exercise 6D

1. 144 seats 2. 251 apples
3. 373 marbles 4. 712 books

Chapter Revision

A. 1. 222 sweets 2. 441 3. 134

B. 1. 323 2. 343 3. 752 4. 260

C. 1. 357 – 150 = 207 2. 498 – 124 = 374
3. 873 – 53 = 820

D. 1.

H	T	O
6	5	4
–	4	4
6	1	0

2.

H	T	O
8	4	3
–	4	0
8	0	3

3.

H	T	O
6	3	5
–	3	1
6	0	4

E. 1. 13 children 2. ₹142

Worksheet

1. 40 2. 50 3. 50 4. 20 5. 30

Reasoning Worksheet 1

1. c. and d. 2. b. and d.
3. a. 4. c. 5. a. and d. 6. c.

Chapter 7

Exercise 7A

1. a. 3 × 4 = 12 b. 4 × 3 = 12
2. a. 7 × 3 = 21 b. 4 × 7 = 28
c. 6 × 4 = 24 d. 3 × 9 = 27
3. a. 3 × 6 = 18 b. 4 × 8 = 32
c. 4 × 5 = 20 d. 9 × 3 = 27

Exercise 7B

2. a. 2 × 3 b. 2 × 5 c. 2 d. 16
e. 60 f. 25 g. 35 h. 0
i. 36 j. 0 k. 24 l. 32
m. 20 n. 20 o. 12
3. a. Multiplier – 2 Multiplicand – 5 Product – 10
b. Multiplier – 7 Multiplicand – 5 Product – 35

Exercise 7C

1. a. 10

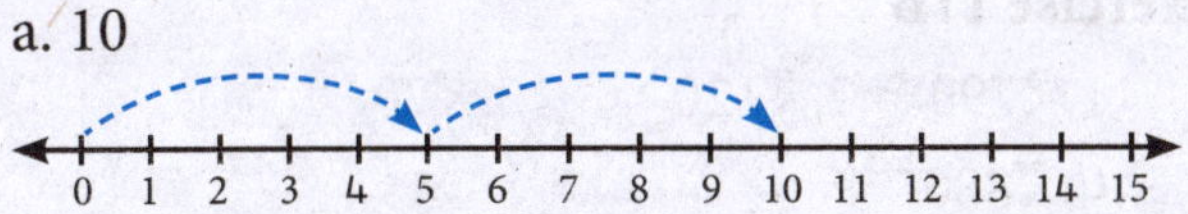

b. 12

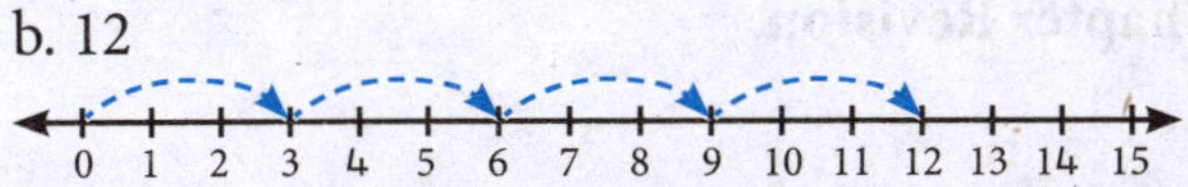

2. a. 14 b. 10 c. 52 d. 660

Exercise 7D

1. 45 2. 50 3. 56 4. 860

Exercise 7E

1. 32 2. 84 3. 96 4. 74 5. 180

Exercise 7F

1. Number of children in 1 row = 6
Number of children in 3 rows = 3 × 6 = 18 children
2. Number of pieces in 1 box = 9
Number of pieces in 5 boxes = 9 × 5 = 45 pieces of cookies
3. Number of shirts sold in 1 month = 323
Number of shirts sold in 2 months
= 323 × 2 = 646 shirts
4. Number of people in 1 train = 230
Number of people in 3 trains = 3 × 230 = 690 people
5. Cost of 1 eraser box = 45
Cost of 6 eraser boxes = 6 × 45 = ₹270

Chapter Revision

A.

	Multiplier	Multiplicand	Product
1.	6	7	42
2.	0	10	0
3.	1	9	9
4.	5	5	25

B. 1. c. 2. a. 3. b. 4. d.

C. 1. 8, 12, 20 2. 14, 28 3. 6, 9
4. 27, 36, 45

D. 1. 24 2. 0, 2, 4, 6 3. 0 and 5 4. 0

E. 1. 60 2. 200 3. 8 4. 15
5. 40 6. 9 7. 0 8. 60

F. 1. 32 sandwiches 2. ₹360 3. 80 people

Worksheet

3 Shirts = ₹660 3 Skirts = ₹690
1 Book = ₹125 2 Pencil Boxes = ₹130
2 Lunch Boxes = ₹156

Chapter 8

Exercise 8A

1. 3 2. 3 3. 4 4. 2 5. 3

Exercise 8B

1. a. 10 b. 6 c. 7 d. 4
2. a. 12 ÷ 4 b. 10 ÷ 5

3. a. 6

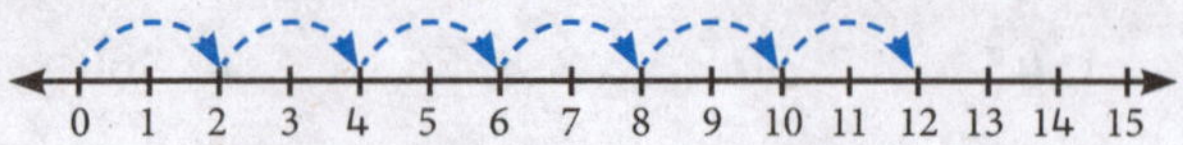

b. 5

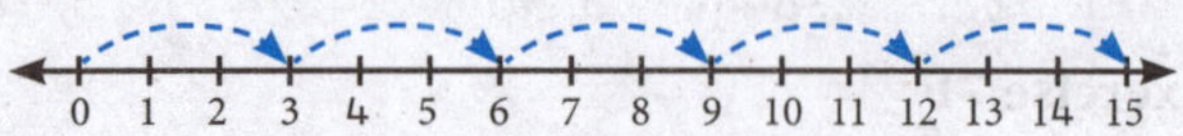

Chapter Revision

A. 1. 3 2. 2 3. 5 4. 4 5. 2, 5

B. 1. T 2. T 3. a. F b. T 4. F
5. T 6. F

C. 1. 2 pages 2. 2 apples 3. 7 packets

Worksheet

1. 2 2. 1 3. 3 4. 1 5. 1

Chapter 9

Exercise 9A

1. metre 2. b., d. 3. b., c., d.
4. a. m b. cm c. m d. m

Exercise 9B

1. a. 2 kg b. 10 g c. 5 g d. 100 g
2. 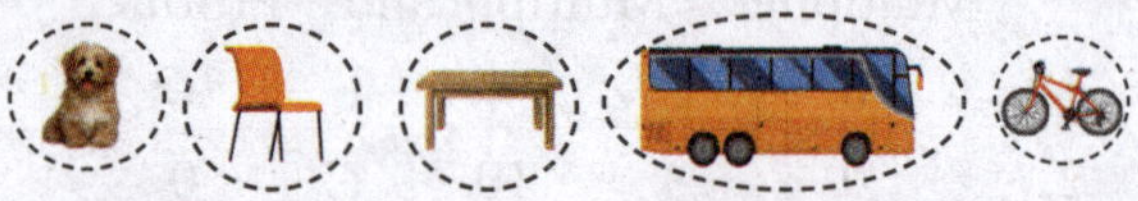
3. a. 1 kg b. 500 g c. 250 g d. 100 g

Exercise 9C

1. a. 5 mℓ b. 1 mℓ c. 250 mℓ d. 20 ℓ
2. Tick (✓) – a., b., d., e. Cross (✗) – c.

Chapter Revision

A. 1. 2 m 2. 7 cm

B. 1. 100 g 2. 9 kg

C. 1. 20 mℓ 2. 5 ℓ

D. 1. m, cm 2. cm 3. g, kg 4. g 5. ℓ

E. 1. longer 2. lighter 3. greater

Worksheet

1. Saif, 109 metres 2. Sachin, 4 glasses of water
3. Anuj, Sachin, Saif 4. a. kg b. mℓ

Chapter 10

Exercise 10A

A. 1. Cloud – C
2. Design on the roof – C
3. Road towards the house – C
4. Rays of the sun – D
5. Side of the door – H
6. Tree trunk – V

Exercise 10B

1. 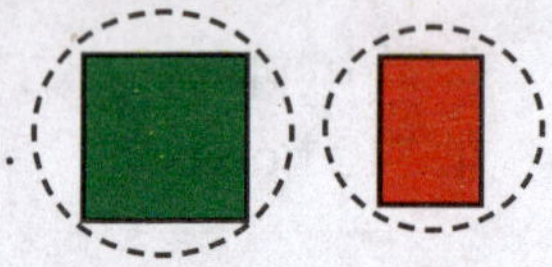 2. 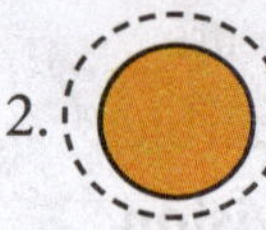

Exercise 10C

1. Globe – Red, Sofa – Pink, Candle – Green, Book – Pink, Pencil Box – Pink, Carton box – Pink, Ball – Red, Pizza slice – Purple, Opened box shown to the right of the ball – Pink, Lamp – Green
2. School bag – Cuboid Battery cell - Cylinder
Eraser – Cuboid
Tissue roll – Cylinder Water bubbles – Sphere
Balloon – Sphere
3. a. S b. R c. S d. R and S
e. R and S f. R and S g. S
h. S i. R and S

Exercise 10D

1.  2.  3. 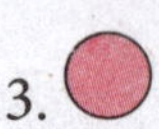 4. 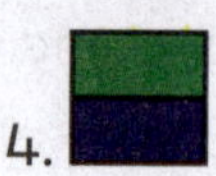

5. 8, 12, 16 6. 14, 16, 18; 2

Chapter Revision

B. 1. F 2. T 3. F 4. T 5. T

C. a. Cuboid b. Cube
c. Cylinder d. Cone
e. Cuboid f. Sphere

D. a. 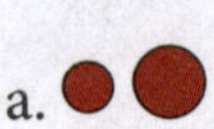 b.  c. B, A
d. X, Y, Z e. 60, 50, 40; 10

Reasoning Worksheet 2

1. d. 2. b. and d. 3. d. 4. b. 5. b. 6. a. 7. d. 8. d. 9. c.

Chapter 11

Exercise 11A

1. a. 60 b. 72 c. 201 d. 600
2. a. < b. > c. = d. >

Exercise 11B

1. ₹790 2. ₹120 3. ₹20
4. ₹880

Chapter Revision

A. 1. < 2. >

B. 1. ₹650 2. ₹16

C. 1. ₹750 2. ₹500 3. ₹214

4. ₹62, combination of notes and coins is ₹50 note, ₹10 note and ₹2 coin. 

Worksheet

A. 2 pencils - ₹30, 3 erasers - ₹30, 2 rulers - ₹40, 1 pencil box - ₹35; Total - ₹155

B. ₹200 or ₹500

Chapter 12

Exercise 12A

1. a. 1:30 b. 7:30 c. 9:30 d. 3:30

2. a.  b. 

c.  d. 

3. a. 8:30 b. 9:00 c. 11:30 d. 1:00, 1:30 e. 2:30

Exercise 12B

1. a. Seven b. Wednesday c. Saturday d. Tuesday e. Friday
2. a. Sunday b. Tuesday c. Thursday d. Sunday
3. Wednesday

Exercise 12C

1. a. March b. July c. February d. November e. June
2. a. April, June, September, November c. autumn d. Summer e. Winter f. pleasant g. monsoon (rainy)
3. a. Summer b. Autumn c. Winter d. Spring e. Monsoon (Rainy)

Chapter Revision

A. 1. 11:30 2. 7 3. Friday 4. Spring

B. 1.  2. 

3.  4. 

C. 1. F 2. T 3. F 4. F 5. F

D. a. January, May, August, October b. Friday c. May d. Sunday

Worksheet

1. Spring, 2 2. Monsoon (Rainy), 4
3. Winter, 1 4. Summer, 3
5. Autumn, 5

Chapter 13

Exercise 13A

1. a. Pencils – 7, Erasers – 6, Pens – 5, Rulers – 4, Notebooks – 3
   b. 25 items c. 4 pencils
   d. Pencils e. Notebooks f. 3
2. a. Red – 4, Yellow – 5, Blue - 2, Green – 2
   b. 13 c. 4 d. 8
   e. 8 cubes and 2 cuboids, that is, 10 f. greater

Chapter Revision

A. 1. 2 dresses 2. 6 pens 3. 5 pens 4. 1 book 5. 2 pairs

B. 1. Monday – 3, Tuesday – 2, Wednesday – 3, Thursday – 4, Friday – 5, Saturday – 6, Sunday – 7
2. 30 3. 2 4. Tuesday 5. Sunday
6. Monday and Wednesday

Worksheet

a. Cartoon b. News c. 9
d. 13 e. 26 f. 12

Reasoning Worksheet 3

1. c. 2. a. and b. 3. d. 4. b.
5. a. No b. Yes c. Thursday d. Yes

Eminent Mathematicians

RADHANATH SIKDAR
(OCTOBER 1813–17 MAY 1870)

He was an Indian Bengali mathematician, who is best known for finding the height of Mount Everest.

JOHANN RAHN
(10 MARCH 1622–25 MAY 1676)

He was a Swiss mathematician, who is known to be the first user of the division symbol (÷) and the therefore sign (∴).

THOMAS HARRIOT
(C. 1560–2 JULY 1621)

He was an English astronomer, mathematician and translator. He is known for introducing symbols for 'is less than (<)' and 'is greater than (>)'.

ROBERT RECORDE
(C. 1512–1558)

He was a Welsh physician and mathematician. He invented the equals sign (=).

MARYAM MIRZAKHANI
(12 MAY 1977–14 JULY 2017)

She was born in Iran. She became the first Iranian student to achieve a perfect score in the International Mathematical Olympiad during her teenage years. She won two gold medals. She is the first female who received the Fields Medal in 2014, the most prestigious award in mathematics. She was a mathematics professor at Stanford University in the U.S. She is considered as one of the greatest mathematicians of recent times.